MOTIVATE
Your **MONEY!**

Plan > Spend > Save > Invest > Gift

MOTIVATE
Your MONEY!

Plan > Spend > Save > Invest > Gift

"Your emotions
should be colorful.
Your finances
should be black and
white."

Mac Gardner, CFP®

Special thanks to our family photographer Amy Garrett (Sweet Pea Photography) for a wonderful cover picture.

Thank you to Julie and Sandra. They played an integral role in bringing my vision to reality.

Table of Contents

Preface

This book has taken some time to put together. It needed time to make the collection of stories...well, a collection. As I toiled away at compiling the stories over the years, I noticed that there were some very strong elements that connected people to their money. The biggest connection was family. A happy and healthy family dynamic helps you to focus on your goals.

I have been supremely blessed to have an amazing family that has supported me in every way imaginable. So, I take this time to thank my grandparents, parents, siblings, aunts, uncles and cousins. They helped to get me where I am today, and I will always be grateful.

I give an even deeper level of gratitude to my wife and my young children. Their laughter and love of life serve as my inspiration to take on any life challenge.

My wife and I decided when we entered into our marriage that we would become each other's PIL (Partner In Life). Her love, support, and encouragement have been unwavering. Thank you, Mama Bear.

MOTIVATIONAL THOUGHTS/NOTES:

_____

_____

_____

_____

_____

_____

_____

_____

_____

_____

_____

_____

_____

_____

_____

MOTIVATE Your **MONEY!**

Plan > Spend > Save > Invest > Gift

Introduction

Ability is what you're capable of doing. Motivation determines what you do. Attitude determines how well you do it.

— LOU HOLZ

What motivates you? Is it your family, your career, your friends? Are you motivated by the desire to learn? Is it fear, or maybe greed? We are all motivated by something or a combination of things. Some people are driven every day by the need to make sure their family is safe and secure. Some are motivated to climb a corporate ladder or by the desire to grow and achieve higher levels of success. Whatever drives you on a daily basis will eventually lead you down that path in life.

I have been motivated for many years to help people manage their financial affairs. As I moved through my career in the financial services industry, I discovered a common thread among people who were very successful in their financial lives: not only were they focused on the financial aspects of their lives, they were motivated to make sure their personal and business affairs were in line with their financial goals.

This may sound like fairly commonplace achievement, but make no mistake: getting your financial affairs aligned with your financial goals is no easy task. You have to work at this process, and work at it for a long time. If you are not motivated to manage your financial affairs, you will find that your finances will try to manage you!

Over the years I have found that there are many benefits to helping people plan the financial aspect of their lives. There is the gratifying feeling that you are contributing to the good of another human being. There is the joy of watching a parent send a child off to college, knowing there will enough money saved to get them all the way through. There is the satisfaction of helping a young business owner open their first venture, and the feeling of accomplishment in helping a business owner in the twilight years fund his ideal retirement.

But I believe the best reward to be gained from helping others is the collection of stories and experiences that are gathered over the years. And once those stories and experiences are collected, the next step is to share them with others, so that we can learn from mistakes and celebrate success.

I remember presenting some financial planning strategies to a group of advisors during a seminar in Florida. One of the advisors interrupted me to say he thought the strategy I was speaking on at the moment was a great idea. "But, he said, "Mac, if you give away your strategies, other people will make money off of them." This could very well be the case.

But here's how I thought about it: If I share a financial planning strategy with someone, what are the odds that they will implement it? The odds are anywhere from 1% to 100%. If I don't share an idea with someone, what are the odds that the strategy will be implemented? 0%. We can all help each other. I help others with my area of expertise, which happens to be financial planning.

As I have moved through the fields of the financial services industry from retail banking to trust administration, to commercial lending, to investment management, to private banking, and now as a wealth manager, my focus has been simple. My role is to gather information, understand needs, desires and goals, then provide guidance to those who need it. This book is a compilation of stories, ideas and experiences that have served to motivate people and help them reach their financial goals and aspirations.

Over the years, I have been blessed with the opportunity to work with numerous people whose levels of wealth span a wide spectrum. I have also had the opportunity to hear and speak with some of the most successful financial advisors in the field. Everyone's financial situation is as unique as their own fingerprints, and every advisor has a unique way of helping their clients.

There is also a consistent common thread that ties together successful financial planning, consistent financial management, and the eventual accomplishment of financial goals. That common thread is motivation. The desire to learn and understand the benefits of financial management leads to the motivation needed to reach your financial goals.

In order for people to get financially motivated, someone needs to serve as a motivator. There needs to be a financial guide or mentor. For most, that person is a parent or teacher. But with the field of financial services becoming increasingly complicated, it is hard for the common citizen to be a specialist in all the many interconnected fields of financial planning. Where do you start? Investments, insurance, taxes, retirement planning, or estate planning? Let's face it, financial planning is complex. And the best advisors are the ones who can take these very complex strategies and make them easy to understand, implement, and monitor.

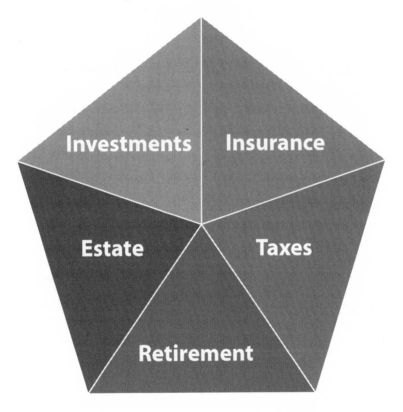

The goal of any great financial advisor is to make sure a financial planning concept or strategy helps their client attain 3 goals. I call it the 3R rule: The concept must be Relatable, Retainable, and Repeatable.

- **Relatable:** the concept must resonate with the person to whom it is being presented. That person must be able to relate to the concept in order to feel comfortable and "buy into" the idea.

- **Retainable:** the idea must also be powerful enough to be able to stay with that person for a period of time.

- **Repeatable:** If the concept is relatable and retainable, guess what? There is a strong possibility that the idea will be repeated to someone else in an attempt to help another person in a similar situation.

Coincidentally, there happens to be a strong correlation between the Relatable, Retainable, and Repeatable idea and the motivation to implement the suggested concept. People are motivated to act when they see there is either a potential for gain or potential to avoid a loss. A true financial advisor ties your needs, wants, fears and dreams to the financial tools and concepts needed to accomplish your lifetime goals. They do this by listening, learning and understanding you. They gather all the strategies and personal stories they have used to help others, and they help you to find the best path to take.

A financial advisor can serve as your personal financial motivator. That's why I decided to write this book. I want to help people to get motivated about their personal financial planning and to help people "Motivate Their Money,"

As I compiled the various concepts, thoughts and strategies for this book, my goal was to ensure that the information passes the Relatable, Retainable, Repeatable test. By presenting financial strategies, concepts and personal stories that resonate with the reader, I intend to help motivate you to take a new approach to managing your personal finances. And if you have already been treading a productive financial path, I hope to reinforce some of the successful actions you have taken in the past.

This book won't be filled with financial planning jargon. It won't be filled with pie-in–the- sky-get-rich-quick schemes. And I assure you that nothing in this book is revolutionary. But what I can promise you is this: the ideas, concepts and strategies in this book have been used by some of the most financially successful people. These are people that I have known personally for years. And the strategies that are discussed have been developed by me with the help of all of those I've had the good fortune of working with over many years of their financial journey. The journey continues. Please enjoy!

Integrity is measured by the distance between your lips and your life.
— MARK SANBORN

CHAPTER 1
Money in Motion

People don't plan to fail;
they fail to plan.

—JOHN L. BECKLEY

Before we jump into the motivational factors behind money and finances, I thought it would be a good idea to do a short history lesson on money and basic economics. I promised in the Introduction that this book would not be filled with financial planning jargon, and I will hold true to that. However, the root of money and how it has come to be in our present day economy should be addressed in any book titled *Motivate Your Money*.

Prior to the invention of money, people used a barter system as a means to transfer assets. Cows, sheep, goods were traded among folks. And as life moved on and our society progressed, people needed a more sophisticated means of handling transactions. Over time, precious metals, coins, and ultimately a banking system were each introduced to serve as a method of transacting business. Then the development of credit came along, and today we live in a society where your ability to manage your debt is monitored daily by various agencies. We have come a long way.

More important than the history of money, though, for the purposes of this book I want readers to get a better understanding of how money flows through our economy, and how we can directly impact the daily money in motion. Money is power. The sooner you realize that simple economic concept, the easier it will be to get motivated about your money. When I say "Money is Power," I mean that money gives us the power over a very important thing in our daily lives. Money will not make you happy. Money will not make you sad. Money is not the root of all evil, nor is it the answer to all your needs. The only thing money provides us is...options. The amount of money we control gives us the power to decide what options are available now and in the future.

The other major focus that I want to touch on in this chapter is the power of choice; more specifically, the power of the financial choices that we make every day and how they can impact your financial future. If you are a sports fan, you may have heard of someone named Herm Edwards. Herm was an NFL player and coach. He is known for his upfront and no-nonsense demeanor when it comes to football and life. Coach Edwards likes to say that "In life, we are all a collection of choices." The choices and decisions that are made each and every day shape the person you are and will be. The choices we make when deciding where to place our power can either lead to a life of financial success or a life of financial ruin.

Let's say you have a $100 bill in your hand. Besides the physical 2.61 by 6.14 inch printed piece of cotton and linen blend paper, what do you have? You have some options. Let's start with the basics. There are only a few things that can be done with money. You can either spend it, save it, invest it, or give it away.

Spend – Save – Invest – Give

The first option that comes to most people's mind when given the $100 bill is what can be purchased. What can I buy with this $100? Why that is the first impulse for most people can be linked to the fact that in our current society we need to spend money to survive. Food, clothing and shelter cost money. We live in a capitalistic society that is driven by profit. I'm not going to go too far down the "capitalism in America" rabbit hole, but the fact that we are bombarded on a daily basis by companies looking to "take your power"—and funnel your hard- earned money in their direction—has created a society of spenders and a culture of unashamed materialism.

And with the relative ease of access to credit, we have seen the insatiable appetite of spending take its toll on families. The insolvency and bankruptcy rates in America have increased significantly over the past 30 years (abiworld.org). We know that we need to spend money. The economy would not survive if enough people did not spend to consume. But how we spend can have life-altering changes for years to come that can affect you and those around you. We will look deeper into the ramifications of our financial decisions in later chapters.

The next option for that $100 is to save it. The concept of saving money is the catalyst for the institution we now know as banks. Many years ago, some innovative people decided to create an entity that would allow them to store or save their valuables. They then realized that with such large sums of valuables on hand, they could make loans and charge a fee for the loan. That fee would in turn be used to pay a rate of return to the owners of the assets held in the bank.

Saving has some great benefits. The concept of paying yourself first from every dollar earned has been espoused by many great thinkers and financial gurus. Saving money allows you to have something to fall back on in case your source of income is either delayed or ended for a period of time. Some believe that you should save 10% of every dollar that is earned. If you ever have the opportunity to read "The Richest Man in Babylon" by George S. Clason, you will understand the 10% rule.

Saving is a key strategy in accomplishing both short term and long term goals. We may be quite aware of the need to save money in a savings account in case of an emergency or a need for access to liquid assets. But there are long term needs in our society that are moving towards being the sole responsibility of the individual.

A case in point is retirement planning, which is one of those long term needs that require a substantial and long term savings strategy. Traditionally, one of the major strategies for meeting this need was the pension; yet fewer companies today are providing their employees with pensions. Over the past 40 years the responsibility for ensuring a financially secure retirement has shifted from the corporation to the individual. Today, retirement plans like the 401(k), 403(b), and IRA are the prevalent tools available to Americans as a means for saving for retirement.

College education planning also requires a long term saving strategy. The cost of a 4- year college education continues to grow at an alarming rate. Savings options like the 529 college savings plan allow for parents to save for their child's education. Starting these types of accounts early in your child's life can provide a source of college funding. Imagine if you started a 529 college savings plan when your child was a year old, and made consistent contributions for 18 years. You would have provided your child with an account to either pay for all four years or at least pay for books.

The third option you have with the $100 is to invest it. There is a common misconception when it comes to the term *invest*. Let's clear the air. Investing is not the same as saving. What's the difference? Investing by definition implies a level of risk. When you save your $100 at a bank or other FDIC insured institution, you expect that you can go to your bank at any time and get your $100 back together with some interest. When you invest your $100, however, you take on the risk of either making money or losing money.

The option to invest the $100 is not a common answer when people are asked what they would do with $100. I believe the reason behind this is a lack of public attention and awareness of the basics of investment management. Children are not exposed in school to terms like mutual funds, stocks, and bonds. Many go through high school and college without any personal financial planning training at all. This lack of exposure has created a level of unease and distrust of anything that resembles an investment.

In response to this, many financial service companies and nonprofit organizations have worked to increase awareness of personal financial planning and how it can benefit our society as a whole. For many years, people relied totally on a financial advisor to help with investment management decisions, but financial service companies are now making information easier to access and allowing people to take a more direct and involved approach to managing their investments.

The last option for that $100 is to give it away. Gifting, or philanthropy, is a way to use your power for the good of others. Many people tithe 10% to their church. Others give to Goodwill or the Salvation Army. I have worked with many families that have accumulated significant levels of wealth; all have given to charitable organizations and have also strategically gifted assets to family members. Gifting allows for the mutual benefit of both parties involved. The giver receives the benefit of knowing that they are helping those in need, while the receiver gets the benefit of a needed asset. There are also tax benefits to gifting, as well as social benefits.

The bottom line is that money was created to serve as a means of transferring ownership of assets or services. The more money you earn, the more options you have. With more options comes more complexity. And with more complexity comes the need for specialized guidance and advice. The financial services industry has expanded enormously over the past few decades as a result of the financial planning needs of our population. As our global economy has grown, billions of people have gained access to more technology, more resources and more capital than ever before.

In the United States alone there is a massive need for expanded education in the field of financial planning. The Baby Boom Generation, Generation X, and now Generation Y are swimming in a sea of financial options with little to no institutional guidance. One of the largest segments of our population that is in need of financial planning services is the Baby Boom Generation. It is estimated that this age demographic is so large that beginning in 2012, 10,000 people will turn 65 each day for the next 20 years!

Your money can work harder for you than you can work for your money. Take advantage of this fact and learn to motivate your money. Learn how money impacts not just you but those around you. Learn how every financial decision you make affects you, not just today but tomorrow. Understand that every dollar you decide to spend, save, invest, and give away impacts your financial path in life, and ultimately decides whether you achieve financial success or financial ruin.

MOTIVATIONAL THOUGHTS/NOTES:

MOTIVATE Your **MONEY!**

Plan > Spend > Save > Invest > Gift

CHAPTER 2

Understanding the 3 F's

*Knowing is not enough;
we must apply. Willing is
not enough; we must do.*

— JOHANN WOLFGANG VON GOETHE

When was the last time you told yourself, "I need to make sure I have enough life insurance to be confident that my family is protected in case of my unforeseen death." Or how about this: "I need to make sure all of my retirement plan accounts are consolidated, in order to avoid any confusion regarding beneficiaries." Or, my all-time favorite: "I need to update my will."

The sad but true fact of the matter is that most people are not proactively managing their financial lives; instead, they turn to an advisor or another financial resource only when something is either wrong or not going well. And when that happens, in many situations a solution isn't found until weeks or months after the problem has arisen. Imagine how much more comforting and fulfilling life would be if we took a pro-active approach to managing our financial lives.

One of the main reasons that people don't take action proactively is fear—either a fear of not knowing the right approach to handling a financial situation, or fear of having to deal with a subject matter that they aren't familiar with. This kind of fear is a powerful emotion, but it can be defeated through exposure and guidance. I have found that once people understand their situation, and recognize that there are numerous ways to overcome their financial hurdles, it is easier to continue down their respective financial path. A large part of financial planning revolves around the emotions and feelings we have about money and the importance one places on the power of financial planning.

The behavioral aspect of financial planning is an area that needs to be focused on in order to truly be motivated to proactively manage your financial lifestyle. Though financial planning is fairly cut and dry, the thing that drives each and every person to make a financial decision is one or more of what I call "life triggers."

These triggers can be marriage, purchasing a home, a new job, a new child, a new business, inheritance, etc. Over the average life span, an individual has numerous large life triggers like these; however, it is actually the little life triggers that can have a profound effect on your financial life and can be the underlying catalysts that determine financial success or failure. Little life triggers are the daily and weekly decisions that are made to determine where and when you place your money. Daily financial habits stretched out over a lifetime can have powerful results, both positively and negatively.

Because of the long term cycle of life, personal financial planning must also be looked at with a long term approach. When someone asks, "How far is the mall?" what is the typical response? Usually someone will reply, "It's 5 miles down the road." Does anyone ever say, "Oh yeah, the mall is 26,400 feet up the road." No one thinks of measuring the driving distance to a destination in terms of feet. We correctly use miles because that is the appropriate unit of measurement.

When dealing with personal financial planning, investing, and retirement planning, it is important to take into consideration that a financial tool that was established when you were 20 can have a dramatic effect on your finances when you are 60. And once that 40 year period has passed, you can't make it up. I'll talk more about the power of compounding interest later in the book.

Now that we have touched on the behavioral aspects of financial planning, as well as life triggers and the long term approach to managing personal finances, let's talk about how they all work together. Every person has walked their own unique path in life. They have a past filled with memories, habits, and the future potential to affect their financial lives and the lives of others. In order to help motivate someone, you need to understand where they're coming from, where they are, and where they want to be. You also need to understand the driving forces that influence them on a daily basis. Is it family, is it career, is it social accomplishment?

Understanding the 3 F's is critical to building the path to financial success. It is also the starting point to help people "motivate their money." When I sit down with a client for the first time, I introduce myself and explain to them how I help people. In order for me to get a better understanding of where they are in life, where they have been and where they want to be, I ask them to tell me about their 3 F's:

FAMILY. FINANCES. FUTURE.

I go through the process of drawing an overlapping three circle venn diagram. Family is the top circle, Finances is the circle to the left, and Future is the circle to the right. This image is used to illustrate the fact that these three aspects of a person's life are indelibly intertwined. Family is placed as the top circle because that is usually the primary driver behind financial decisions. Finances are placed to the left to illustrate that financial decisions drive the Family unit. And Future is placed to the right to illustrate the forward direction of the family and finances working together.

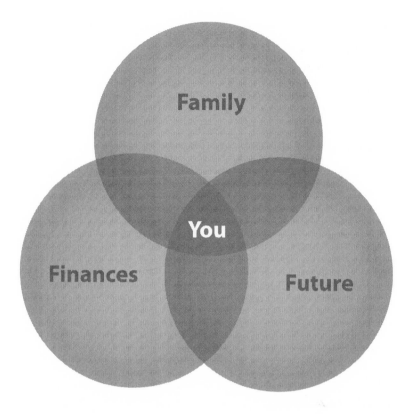

Family

The first F, Family is the starting point. Money is worthless if it cannot provide options to you and those whom you hold dear. If you are married with children, it is very likely that your financial motivation lies within the needs to make sure your spouse and children are safe and secure. Each dollar of income that enters that household goes toward providing for that family unit. Be it paying for a mortgage, food, family events, vacations, school, the list goes on. The other financial planning concerns for a family with children are life insurance, disability insurance, a college 529 plan, and retirement plans for further down the road. These are the concerns of that individual family unit, and some of the financial tools that can serve to benefit them. But what is the true motivation of a parent?

If we dig deeper into the family unit, we see that the financial motivation is to provide for both the short term and long term benefit of those in the family. We have all heard our parents say, "I want to provide my children with opportunities and options that I didn't have." Each generation wants the next generation to move ahead and gain an advantage over the prior generation. We want our children to be smarter, more exposed, and to take advantage of the fruits of our labor.

The million dollar question is: Are you providing the next generation with the best personal financial management skills? If you are not motivating your money, it is extremely difficult for those around you to successfully motivate their money. The family unit is both the seed of inspiration and the future motivation for financial success. If we can inculcate good financial habits into both the big and little triggers in our financial lives, we can then share them with those in our family circle and others that we influence on a regular basis.

Family influence and outreach is another fascinating aspect of personal financial planning and financial motivation. Many times, when advisors work with their clients they will focus solely on the client's immediate family needs. What I have found in my years of financial advising is that although it can be easy to systematically focus our energies on those in the direct family circle, this doesn't mean that those outside the direct family will not and cannot have an effect on the finances of those within it.

By going just one step around an individual through what I call the "Up, Down, and Around" method, we can help to uncover potential financial influences. I draw the following diagram inside the Family circle: I draw a smaller concentric circle. Inside the smaller circle is the client. If they are married, the spouse is included in the circle. Then we go Up, and talk about the parents. Next we go Down, and talk about children (if any). And finally, we go Around and I ask about siblings.

I routinely ask the following family questions to get a better understanding of how family and extended family work to influence financial decisions:

- *Are your parents still with us?*

- *Do your parents live close by?*

- *Do you have children (grandchildren)?*

- *Do your children (grandchildren) live close by?*

- *Do you have any siblings?*

- *Do your siblings live close by?*

- *Do you foresee the need to have a financially dependent relative (mother, father, and sibling)?*

- *Do you foresee a family inheritance?*

After we have gone through the "Up, Down, and Around" process, I explain my rationale for the questions. Though we can proactively plan for the foreseen goals and potential pitfalls in life, there are unforeseen obstacles that can have a dramatic effect on personal finances.

The last 2 questions drive home the reasons for expanding the knowledge of the immediate family unit and the potential impact that it can have on achieving family goals. Many people plan to save for retirement. Many save for their child's college expenses. But how many people purposely save for an adult spendthrift brother/sister? How many save up for a parent who has become incapacitated or is suffering from Alzheimer's disease? How many save up for an adult child who's experiencing a costly divorce? How many know what to do when they receive a windfall of money from a deceased relative? These issues can arise over a lifetime.

By understanding the family dynamics, we can see a more comprehensive picture of the past, present and future financial needs. We also get a greater insight into financial habits, concerns and issues. This information will serve as the foundational building blocks that pave a pathway to financial success.

Once you determine the "who" that needs to benefit from financial planning, the next step is to determine the "why". Why should you be motivated to make sure your financial well-being is safe, secure and on track?

Here are some of the most popular questions I present to people to help them get to the "why" in their own lives:

- **Who is dependent on the financial decisions you make every day?**

- **What financial steps have you taken to ensure your family will be secure over the next 5 years, 10 years, 20 years and more?**

- **How comfortable are you and your spouse when it comes to making big financial decisions?**

- **What is your process when it comes to managing your financial assets?**

- **If either you or your spouse were to die, how would your finances look?**

- **If you were to die tomorrow, would your surviving family be able to manage their financial affairs?**

Though the answers to these questions differ from person to person, there is a consistent theme that connects every answer. They all require some sort of financial plan to be in place to ensure success.

The "why" for many financial concerns is usually firmly based in the need to provide security for ourselves and loved ones. And if we dig deeper we will see that by security, we mean the ability to provide those closest to us with as many life options as can be afforded.

Notice that I have not mentioned any financial products in this section of the book. The true purpose of a financial advisor or financial guide is to learn first and understand. Then, second, to analyze the situation, suggest solutions and then implement the plan. This process is essential to motivating your money.

Finances

The next F that needs to be understood by the client I am talking with is Finances. When I use the term *finances,* in this context, I speak about all the assets that make up the estate of the individual or family. I will draw another diagram that lists Assets, Liabilities, Income, and Expenses. We are now moving away from the subjective discussion of family dynamics to the objective topic of what the current financial picture looks like.

It's important to remember that although we are now moving into an area of objective information involving account values and property valuations, we still are in the domain of behavioral finance. There is always a story behind every financial asset that a person either purchases or invests in. I make it a habit to ask a very simple question when reviewing financial assets: "Tell me about that account." You'd be surprised how those 5 simple words phrased like a question can evoke some deep and unexpected answers.

By better understanding the reasons why a financial product was purchased, it is easier to piece together a financial timeline. This timeline provides an insight into what is and was a priority in that person's life at the time of the purchase. Everything in your financial portfolio should have a purpose. And more importantly, you should always know what that purpose is.

Here are some typical questions I ask people when reviewing their financial assets:

- **What purpose does that financial asset serve in your life?**
- **Was it a need, a want or a desire?**
- **Did the financial solution meet expectations?**
- **Who suggested the product?**
- **What did the product cost?**
- **How long have you owned it?**
- **How did you go about choosing the product?**
- **What's your process in managing the account?**
- **How do you determine or measure the success of the account?**

Uncovering the stories behind financial assets provides us with not only an overall picture of financial net worth, but more importantly, a behavioral insight into the habits of the owner. I often joke with my clients at this point, telling them we're going to work on cleaning up their "financial attic." Like any product or service we buy throughout our lifetime, financial service products are usually acquired to fulfill an immediate need. One of the big differences, however, is that if left unattended and "stowed away," a financial asset can out-live its purpose, become a costly burden, or even provide an unintended benefit. Either way, the purpose behind the pieces that make up the financial picture must be uncovered in order to get a true understanding of current and future goals.

I have worked with clients who are extremely conservative and are content with owning financial products which occupy that spectrum of the risk scale. A vast majority of their financial assets are held in bank vehicles like savings accounts and CD's. They pine over the interest rates of the 1980's and they have no desire to "invest in the market." The people who fit this type of profile have little to no debt, and have worked all of their lives while living under their means. Not surprisingly, these people's parents were conservative in nature and likely were part of the Great Depression era commonly known as the Silent Generation.

I have also worked people who believe the only way to grow capital is to take risk, a lot of risk. Investment vehicles are inherently filled with risk; some, such as currency trading, commodities and derivatives, can entail considerable risk. They were created to provide a market for growth and to hedge against certain market volatility. Compared to the investments favored by the strictly conservative investor, these are on the other end of the risk scale. You can make a lot of money, and you can lose a lot of money.

A majority of people have some combination of stocks, bonds, mutual funds, annuities, and bank products in their "financial attic." Real estate holdings, commodities and ownership in business interests are also common holdings. A key factor in putting the pieces of the financial puzzle together is properly aligning risk tolerance, time horizon, and asset structure. I believe that having proper symmetry among these elements represents the "guardrails" on your financial path.

Here's what I mean: Many planners believe that we should have short term, mid-term, and long term goals. Some use what is called a "bucket strategy" to illustrate these three goals. Short Term goals (1 to 3 year time period) are usually financed by products that are not very risky, such as checking accounts, savings accounts and CD's; they don't earn much but there is little to no volatility in these types of products.

Mid Term goals (4 to 7 years) can be financed with a variety of financial products. The key for this bucket is to realize that a little more risk can be taken due to the longer time horizon, but this bucket will eventually be used to "pour over" assets into the Short Term bucket. So too much risk can't be taken in the Mid Term bucket to jeopardize the overall flow of assets from one bucket to another.

The Long Term goal bucket can include an even greater variety of financial assets. Stocks, bonds, mutual funds, ETF's, and real estate are the typical types of assets that can be found in the Long Term bucket. Because the time frame for this bucket is longer, one could benefit from taking more risk because there's more time for potential growth, and more time to recover from potential loss.

As you sit down and complete an inventory of your financial assets, try utilizing the three-bucket approach yourself and gauge how your financial assets are constructed. There is no absolute wrong way to manage your financial assets, just as there is no absolute right way. The issues that arise when people are trying to manage on their own are often a product of misinformation, or a misunderstanding of the proper expectations of results. CD's are not bad financial tools, just as gold is not the best financial asset, and stocks are not the answer to every investment question. Some folks swear by the need to own real estate, while others feel that annuities are the best income-generating tools in the market. Understanding the short term and long term risks and benefits involved in each and every financial asset is the key to structuring a financial plan that will work for you, and with you, for years to come.

Once we have an understanding of the family dynamic and how financial assets are structured, we have a picture of what is going on now and what has happened in the past. The next step is to talk about the Future. This aspect of planning is the most fulfilling. Many times I will ask a client, "If you could wave a magic wand, what would you like to have financially accomplished in 5 years?" Asking the question in this manner allows you to answer without the constraint of what the current limitations may be. Notice I didn't ask, "If you stay on the path you're on now, where do you think you'll be financially in 5 years?" The neat thing about the future is that we can control it with the financial choices we make. I want you to think about your goals in a way that allows you to not only see it, but to verbalize it and even write it down.

Granted, some goals are possible and some goals are probable. It's important to differentiate which ones are which. It's also important that we put realistic expectations on the time horizons wherein we expect to reach or exceed our goals. Once a financial goal is established and a time frame for the goal is determined, it's also important to attach a "what if" to that goal. By "what if" I mean, what if I get to the goal ahead of time? Or, what if I don't get to the goal in time? What will my plan look like? We know those immortal words spoken by those who endure challenges in life (which is everyone): Life Happens! What is the contingency plan if your original plan doesn't work?

If we go back to the three-bucket system for segmenting goals and correlating the best asset to fund the respective goals, we can list the goals under each bucket. A short term goal may be to pay off a credit card. That would be best serviced by a liquid cash account or savings account. You may also achieve this goal using cash flow from your current income. A mid-term goal may be to take a dream family vacation. That could be funded by an investment account that is allocated in a manner that provides some growth with minimal volatility. A long term goal, like saving for college or retirement, would benefit from a tax advantaged account such as a college 529 plan or a 401(k) plan.

Knowing the right type of account to fund in order to reach a goal is a great first step. The big challenges to personal financial planning, though, are deciding which account gets priority over which, and how to make all the accounts work together over a long period of time. It would be great to put a chunk of money into each bucket for each goal and sail off into the sunset of an ideal retirement. But we all work with a finite amount of income and many people do not have the large amounts of capital needed to fund all of our buckets in one shot. This means that we need to make sure that our ever-changing lives, finances and goals are consistently in line with our personal financial plans. It's not an easy task, but the benefits are amazing!

Future

One of the best and most appropriate observations I've heard on the subject of planning for the future was made by a former colleague of mine who was commenting on retirement. He was quoted in a financial news article as saying, "We all know with 100% certainty what we are retiring from, but we have no idea what we are retiring to." Setting a financial plan for the future takes a lot of work, and it also takes a lot of patience.

We can lay out the best plan based on the information we have today, but no one truly knows with 100% certainty what will happen in the future. Our main guide when it comes to planning for the financial future is statistical probability. And just as there is a probability of everything in our lives going just right, there's also a probability that things out of our control can have a derailing effect on our financial lives.

When I sit with clients and ask them to tell me about their future goals, I get a myriad of answers. Depending on where they are in their respective life cycles, the answer could be: buy a home, pay off debt, send the kids to college, retire comfortably, or pass assets on to their heirs. Every person's view of their future self is unique, and for the most part, positive. Everybody has the best intentions of working toward their future goals. However, if you were to reference any news source, you would read that many Americans cannot afford to buy a home, cannot afford to go to college, or have not saved enough for retirement. So the question that naturally comes up is, "Why don't more people reach their future financial goals?"

My answer to that question is simple. A vast majority of people in America haven't been prepared from an early age to practice sound personal financial planning—a subject that isn't even offered in most elementary, middle, or high schools. Sadly enough, many students don't even get exposure to personal financial planning strategies in college. So if there is no financial planning guidance, no good financial habits to emulate, no personal financial planning exposure, how can you tip the scales of financial success in your favor? The answer is simple. You can't.

The first step to reaching a financial goal, whether short term or mid-term, is to have a financial plan. After I hear the future goals of my clients and we talk about how great those goals are, and how wonderful life will be once they get there, I then do my job as a financial advisor. I help them bring together their dreams and their reality. I help them to determine if their dream can become a reality. And if they are true to their vision of financial reality, they can attain their future goals. My job isn't to provide my clients with dreams and endless possibilities. My job is to provide my clients with sound financial planning based on current facts and likely probabilities.

Here are a few questions I ask folks when discussing financial plans for the future:

- *Have you ever developed a plan for your goal?*

- *Once you've implemented your plan, what will be its possible effects on your current financial situation?*

- *How will you know if your plan is on track?*

- *If you don't reach your goal, how will that impact you and your family?*

We can add some clarity to the overall financial picture—and begin to do some earnest planning—once we have prioritized the family needs/goals and aligned them to the appropriate financial tools and strategies. So far, we have discussed planning for welcomed and expected goals. More specifically, we have a addressed goals that deal with growing assets over the short, mid term and long term to attain those goals.

But what about those unexpected issues that arise throughout life? Loss of income, disability, and premature death are aspects of planning for the future that, sadly, many people overlook. Though it's nice to discuss future goals of sending the kids off to college or flying the family to Antigua for that dream beach vacation, it's also financially disingenuous to only plan for the potential good that can happen in life.

Planning for the unexpected is, metaphorically speaking, the other side of the financial planning coin. It is imperative, when you discuss future financial goals, that risk management be at the top of mind. The concept of risk versus reward must be applied to every financial decision that is made. Every time you use your power, it has both a short term and long term effect on your ability to reach your financial goals. Keep a mindset of asking yourself two important questions:

- If I act on this and use my money this way, what is both the short term and long term benefit?

- How can this choice harm my financial plan and stop me from achieving my goals?

The financial services industry has evolved over time to provide financial services that answer to the needs to a constantly demanding market. If there is a financial problem that exists, there's a very good chance that some company has created a tool or product that will either alleviate or mitigate the risk. And if it doesn't exist yet, don't worry — someone somewhere is probably already thinking about it. These products have a cost and sometimes they can cost a lot. But part of proactive financial planning includes weighing the cost versus the benefit of using our money.

Insurance was created to provide capital in case of the unexpected. It is used to either manage, mitigate or eliminate risk. Homeowner's and auto insurance protect our homes and automobiles in case of unexpected damage or loss. Life insurance provides capital in case of unexpected death. Income annuities were created to provide income in case you live too long. Long Term Care insurance was created to pay for care in later life. Disability insurance was created to replace income due to injury. Some companies have developed hybrid products to help serve multiple purposes.

The litany of financial service products has created a double edged sword for the consumer to contend with. Today there are multiple companies and resources available to help you manage any conceivable financial issue. But the constant evolution and subsequent complexity of the industry has also made it more confusing for the average consumer to easily find the best solution.

That's why it is so important, when undertaking the personal financial planning process, that we intimately understand how Family, Finances and Future work — and then how they work together. This overall concept will be the guiding force that helps to build the path that guides your journey to and through financial success.

MOTIVATIONAL THOUGHTS/NOTES:

_____

_____

_____

_____

_____

_____

_____

_____

_____

_____

_____

_____

_____

_____

_____

_____

_____

MOTIVATE Your **MONEY!**

Plan > Spend > Save > Invest > Gift

CHAPTER 3
Five Steps to Financial Success

*Stay committed to your
decisions, but stay flexible
in your approach.*

— TOM ROBBINS

David Bell is one of the best personal financial planners I know. He's probably forgotten more about financial planning than most advisors know! The first time I met David was many years ago, when I was a wholesaler. To this day I can see him in front of a roomful of people, standing next to his white flip board with a marker in hand. Of all his financial planning wisdom, the most profound concept I remember from David's presentation was one that began with 3 simple letters he wrote on the board: K L T.

Before he wrote those letters he asked a question: "What are three elements that are needed to begin a mutually beneficial relationship?" We all sat there thinking about it, and he let us go through all sorts of guessing games. The answer is simple, profound and applies to almost every relationship: In order to enter a beneficial relationship with someone, you need to Know, Like, and Trust that person.

If you step back and think about it, he's absolutely right. When you're looking for, let's say, a contractor to repair your home, how does the process start? You may ask a friend or family member if they KNOW anyone. The follow-up question is almost always, "Did they do a good job?" This is another way of asking if they LIKED the job that was done. And after all the due diligence is done and you are ready to sign on the contract, you make a conscious decision that this person is competent and worthy to get the job done. You TRUST that the contractor will do the same kind of job they did before.

The Know, Like and Trust method doesn't just work for contractors. It applies to all types of relationships, business, personal, and otherwise. Think about your current relationship. You met this person through someone or somewhere that you know. To keep the relationship going you probably liked this person. And you have decided to trust this person with your thoughts, feelings, and much more.

After hearing David Bell speak and tell us about K L T, I expanded the concept to include three other letters: C P R. I called the resulting six-letter combination the "Get In / Stay In" concept. We know what it takes to enter a relationship: Know, Like and Trust. But once you're there, what does it take to *stay* in a mutually beneficial relationship? I posited that it also takes three key elements: Communication, Productivity and Respect.

Get In

Know

Like

Trust

Stay In

Communication

Productivity

Respect

If we stay with our contractor analogy, we can see how Communication, Productivity and Respect work to maintain a healthy relationship. First, there needs to be constant COMMUNICATION between you and the contractor to ensure that the project is complete to the satisfaction of both parties. The reason for hiring the contractor is to PRODUCE a desired result. If the contractor does keep up their end of the bargain or if you don't pay as agreed, there's going to be a problem.

The third element is the glue that keeps these components together. Both parties must RESPECT each other and the understanding of their respective roles. The contractor is a specialist in what they do. Their service is a commodity that is needed by the homeowner. The homeowner has the capital and the desire for a specific result. Both must work together and respect the needs, wishes and desires of the other for the project to be successful.

I have shared my "Get In / Stay In" concept of relationship building with nearly every client I have worked with. My point in sharing this story is to illustrate to the client how I view my role in their lives and how I expect them to view me.

It gives us both an understanding of what we are both trying to accomplish by having me in their lives.

I also ask that they relate the KLT / CPR concept to their personal finances. We all have a relationship with money. We Know it, we Like to have it, and we Trust that when we use it we won't have any surprises from the person we're transacting business with. But have you developed a mutually beneficial relationship with your money? Ask yourself the following questions:

- *Do you really know the true power and purpose behind your money?*

- *Have you ever looked at why you like doing what you do with your money?*

- *Do you believe that you have enough information about personal financial planning to reach your goals?*

- *Do you honestly communicate with your financial plan?*

- *What does your money produce for you on a daily, weekly, monthly, yearly basis?*

- *Do you respect your own ability to manage your finances and reach your financial goals?*

Building a better relationship with your money is a critical first step in being able to motivate your money. The better you understand what you need and how to get there, the easier it is to build the path to success.

One of the biggest benefits of working in the financial services industry for a lengthy period of time is that you get the opportunity to hear a lot of stories of success. You also get to hear a lot of stories of failure. After working with clients from all phases of the financial planning life cycle, I began to see some startling similarities in the stories of those who were financially successful well into their later stages of life. There were some basic ground rules that were followed by the most successful families. These people did not start off wealthy. They didn't have large amounts of money to begin with. They didn't inherit millions of dollars from wealthy parents. So what was the secret to their financial success?

If we go back to our $100 bill exercise, you'll remember that there are only a few things that can be done with money. You can either: spend it, save it, invest it or give it away. With those options in mind, we then have to look at the common thread that ties these functions of money together. As I worked with people over the years I would continually hear some common themes in the lives and stories of those who had achieved financial success. The common elements became the basic building blocks for my "5 Steps to Financial Success." The people who have created a mutually beneficial relationship with their money that has led them on a path to financial success have followed these 5 steps:

Step 5: Gift Generously

Step 4: Invest Wisely

Step 3: Save Diligently

Step 2: Spend Cautiously

Step 1: Plan Accordingly

The "5 Steps to Financial Success" follow in a chronological order for a reason. If you don't have a plan, you might as well tell yourself that you are not reaching your goal. Not that it's impossible to reach a goal without a plan, but it's highly improbable. If you don't have a thorough understanding of how your money is being spent, or you haven't set a budget, it is difficult to spend cautiously. Spending cautiously means that you're keenly aware of where you place your power. You intimately know the where, when, why, and how your money behaves. If you can't spend cautiously, and in fact overspend or live beyond your means, you can't get to Step 3, which is saving diligently. However, if you can master Step 2 and live beneath your means, you will be able to progress to Step 3 and begin a consistent habit of Saving Diligently.

Some believe that you should always pay yourself first, suggesting that 10% of every dollar earned should go into a savings vehicle. By making saving a consistent part of your financial process you will then be able to move up to Step 4, Investing Wisely. This is the most complex of the 5 Steps. Having someone who can help to guide you in this field will prove to be extremely beneficial. Though emotions may drive our financial habits, they do not drive the world of investments. So having an objective resource that can help you to focus on your investment strategies and goals is key to making Step 4 work.

Step 5, Gifting Generously, can be done at any time. I place it as the last step only because the prior steps have a greater impact on overall financial success. Giving is important. We frequently see acts of altruism carried out by some of the wealthiest people in the world. They have amassed large amounts of wealth and they feel it is a good thing to "give back." Even if you are not wealthy, giving generously is a way to help others who are in need, and it gives you a feeling that you've made a financial impact on another's life.

Now, let's discuss each step in greater detail.

STEP 1. PLAN ACCORDINGLY

Every financial success story I have ever heard started with a plan. Not just any arbitrary plan, but a plan that was structured according to the goal in mind. Whether the goal was buying a home, purchasing a car, paying for college, you name it, there was some sort of strategy that was followed which allowed a person to manage, monitor, and measure the path to accomplishment.

Notice that *Plan* Accordingly is the first step on the path to financial success. It's not "dream accordingly" or "wish accordingly." When dealing with personal financial planning, it is imperative to realize that every financial goal you can conceive needs to have a correlated financial plan. A strategy or concept by itself is not a plan. A great thought is not a plan. A plan is a combination of a well-thought-out *strategy* combined with the specific *tactics* that will be utilized over a specified *period of time* that will be needed to accomplish a goal. A plan is not set in stone, but rather, like our personal lives, will change. There will be contingencies, changes, and hurdles along the way. That's what makes personal financial planning so important and yet so much more complicated than it may seem at first.

If we look at 3 of the most common financial goals of the average American family, we can see just how complicated Step 1 can be. Home ownership is a common financial goal. Some statistics show that 67% of Americans own their home. Why isn't this higher? Why is it that only ⅔ of the American population own a home? There's more that goes into owning a home than just building a house and moving into it.

In our present-day financial environment, homes cost a considerable amount of money. And if you want to buy a home and you don't have all the money on hand, you need to take out a loan. And if you want that loan, you need to qualify for that loan. So the steps needed to buy a home may include having enough for a down payment and having a good credit score that would qualify you for a loan.

Now, if we were to look up the average age of a first-time home buyer, we'd see that age 31 would be the average age. If you started working at age 18, we would presume a span of approximately 13 years of financial decisions between your first job and when you would buy your first home. A lot of financial planning can be done in 13 years. A lot of good behaviors and mutually beneficial decisions between you and your money can be developed in 13 years. But why do only 67% of Americans own a home? Because while some people do sit down and devise a plan to budget and develop a savings strategy, there are many people who do not.

Another common goal that many families have is paying for college. If you went to college and have children, you know personally that the cost of a college education is increasing dramatically every year. Many parents would like to be able to provide assistance to their children by paying for some, or all of their college education. The belief in giving the next generation a hand up, or giving them opportunities that the prior generation didn't have, is a strong driver behind this goal.

With the cost of higher education ever-increasing, the likelihood of needing to take a loan to finance college has become a concern for both the parent and the child. The government has created college savings plans to provide a financial vehicle that can help families save for their child's college education. If we presume that the average age of a college freshman is 18, and that the only requirement to start a college savings plan is the child's Social Security number, we can say that we have an 18-year window to give us time to save and reach the goal of providing funds for college.

A lot of financial planning can be done in 18 years! But the fact is that few people are aware of what are called 529 College Savings Plans. These plans allow you to save for your child's college expenses in a tax-advantaged account. The assets grow in a tax-deferred account, and as long as the distributions are made to cover qualified educational expenses, the money comes out tax-free, too.

One of the biggest life goals for most Americans centers around retirement. This is the area of financial planning that I have specialized in for many years. Comprehensive retirement planning covers two main phases: the accumulation phase and the distribution phase. If you thought homeownership goals and college savings goals were complicated, prepare yourself for one of the biggest and most complicated challenges our society will be having in the years to come.

The idea of "Retirement" in our society has fundamentally changed over the last few decades. In 1950 the average retirement age was 65, and life expectancy then was 70. If we look at modern times, the retirement age may have stayed the same — but life expectancy is closer to 85. So, in a little over 50 years we have gone from 5 years in retirement to 15 years. That seismic shift has led to some serious ramifications in the field of retirement planning. If we combine this element of longevity with historically low national savings rates and the massive reduction in corporate sponsored pensions, we have a potential recipe for disaster.

So, starting your retirement plan from Dollar 1 earned at age 18, and extending it past the start of retirement at age 65 all the way to death at age 85 gives you close to 70 years to plan. There are countless financial decisions that will be made during that lifetime. And every choice has both a short term and long term effect on reaching your goals. If there is no clear financial plan established to reach your retirement plan goal, you will end up like the millions of Americans that will not be able to retire in the way they imagined. Or even worse, they might not be able to retire at all.

Having the right plan for the right goal is Step 1. Once the blueprint for the journey is sketched out, we can then begin to lay the stones that will pave the path for the lifetime journey towards the numerous financial goals we set for ourselves. These stones will be made of financial decisions we make each and every day of our lives. Some of these decisions are small, like how much to spend on buying lunch. Some will be big, like how much house I can afford to buy. Big or small, these decisions work together to build your financial path in life.

STEP 2. SPEND CAUTIOUSLY

This step is the mortar in your financial path through life. The spending process is fluid, but once the moment of a financial interaction has passed, it has a permanent effect on your current financial path. It will also affect your financial future. How you spend money, and the repercussions of those financial choices, can either lead you down a financial path filled with good options or a life filled with options you would rather not have to deal with.

Think of your money like a flowing stream of water. A stream of water can be a hugely beneficial asset. If channeled correctly it can provide for irrigation, supply power, and serve as a means of supporting life. If channeled incorrectly, that stream of water can cause catastrophic damage. It can destroy a home, a village or an entire city. It's important that your cash flow is working for your benefit and not leading you down a path of financial destruction.

Every dollar you earn and possess comes to you through a stream called the global economy. Our capitalistic system is driven by how money flows and who is benefiting the most from the flow of that capital. The fact that you're reading this book indicates you've either had a job or owned a business as a means to earn a living. You probably worked very hard to make sure you got a raise, or worked hard to make sure that your business becomes more profitable. You know that the more money you make, the more options you have in life. For many, the major focus in financial planning is on the income side of the ledger. But is your focus on the expense side of your life as detailed? Do you really sit down and try to uncover the why, what, when, and how behind your expenses? Do you spend cautiously?

Many of us have heard the old adage, "Living below your means." But what does that really mean? Simply put, it means that if you earn $100 a week, you should try to maintain your lifestyle by only spending between $50 and $90. The rest should go towards building up a savings account. This may look easy, but we all know that it's a lot easier said than done.

The reason why it's easier said than done is that we live in a society that encourages spending. Think about how many times in a day you come in contact with some advertisement wanting you to buy a product or service. You wake up and there are commercials on TV and the radio pushing something on you. Then you check your email and there's tons of spam. And don't forget the drive in to the office; billboards are screaming at you about some new product that must be had.

Setting a budget is the first step to mastering the Spend Cautiously phase. The next, and even more important step is sticking to that budget. Your budget is the fuel that drives your financial engine. Your spending habits determine if you can reach your short term and long term goals. Simply put, if you don't properly fuel your financial engine, you won't get far.

Imagine you're planning a wonderful road trip and you've done all the prep work. Car is packed, kids are packed, GPS has all the settings, you're good to go. But you only have a half tank of gas, instead of the full tank you need. You can imagine how much fun the trip will be. Likewise, if your financial engine isn't being fed with a high premium budget, your financial journey through life may be filled with a lot of stops on the side of the road to repair and refill. Even worse, you may not be able to reach your desired destination.

If you fall into the habit of overspending, guess what? There are a ton of credit card companies that would be more than happy to issue you a line of credit that can potentially over-leverage you and keep you on a path of insolvency. Owing more than you own throughout your lifetime is a sure way to go broke and make other people rich off of your hard earned money. And that is a sad and unfortunate fact for millions of people.

STEP 3. SAVE DILIGENTLY

Mastering Step 2 is essential to moving up to Step 3. Simply put, if you can't spend cautiously and live below your means, it's almost impossible to save. Saving diligently simply means that before you pay anyone else, you pay yourself first. There is a great book that was written many years ago, called "The Richest Man in Babylon" by George Samuel Clason. One of the basic premises of the book is the notion that of every dollar that is earned, 10% must be saved. By paying yourself before you pay anyone else, you're ensuring that you have assets saved for a rainy day.

The concept of saving is as old as humanity. You may have heard the common saying, "Spend for today and Save for tomorrow." The statement is not totally accurate, but the point still holds. Saving allows us to have a backup of assets in case the unexpected happens. Bad crops can wreak havoc on a farmer. It would be even worse if he didn't have grain stored and saved for just such an occasion. From a personal financial planning perspective, saving allows you to store assets in case of unexpected income loss, unforeseen expenses, or for future capital goals.

We endlessly hear that we should save for a rainy day, or save for college or save for retirement. As we move along our path to financial success, we must truly take advantage of the power of saving and the various financial vehicles that have been created to allow us to conveniently save. Saving allows you to take advantage of the power of compounding. Saving allows you to reach your short term and long term goals. Saving allows you to feel psychologically secure about your financial future.

Now that we have moved up to Step 3, we cannot forget to take into account how Steps 1 and 2 fit into our plan. Remember that Step 1, Plan Accordingly is the constant driver of the total personal financial plan. It determines if the goal is either short term, mid-term, or long term. The time frame of the goal will in turn determine the best saving strategy and financial vehicle to use in order to achieve the goal.

Many financial planners believe that you should have anywhere between 6 months to a year of income saved in a liquid account. This can be funded by utilizing either a savings account, money market or CD. This type of short term savings goal should have little or no risk associated with it, because it will need to be accessed for a short term need.

Mid-term and long term savings goals such as vacations, automobiles, home or retirement can be funded with a variety of financial product accounts. The main considerations when saving for longer term goals are risk tolerance and time horizon. An individual's risk tolerance is as unique as ones fingerprints. That tolerance for risk must be properly aligned with the required time horizon to ensure that the appropriate financial strategies and tools are utilized.

STEP 4: INVEST WISELY

This is the next step to financial success. I want to draw a clear line of demarcation when it comes to saving versus investing. There is a big difference between the two. Though a saving strategy may include investment vehicles, saving by definition is not investing. Investing inherently includes a level of risk. Saving should not.

Another misconception that people have about investing is the comparison to gambling. You may have heard people say, "I don't invest in the stock market, it's like gambling money." This could not be further from the truth. The basic difference between gambling and investing is control. When you go to Las Vegas and step up to the roulette wheel, you have no control over where that little white ball drops. The odds of your walking out with less money than you came in with are greatly in favor of that casino.

Over the long term, the odds of making money as a professional gambler are even smaller. Granted, there are chances that the quarter you dropped into the one-arm bandit could pay out a million dollars, but you'd have better odds of being struck by lightning a few times in a year. When it comes to gambling, the only control you have is the ability to give away your money, in hopes of getting something back.

Investing—and more specifically, investing over a long period of time— is not gambling. You can control where your money goes, and you can influence your expected rate of return by investing in numerous types of financial vehicles. Some investments are created to provide long term capital appreciation, some to provide income. Some investments are created to do both.

You have the opportunity to allocate your investment assets in a way that will allow you to feel comfortable with how your money grows over time. You can control the decision to own whichever type of investment will provide an expected range of return that will allow you to achieve your financial goals. You're not that lucky when it comes to gambling.

Investing allows you to participate in the growth of the economy. In fact, investing is the engine that drives capitalism. The basic premise behind investing is a concept of risk versus reward. If an investment has an inherently high amount of risk, there is a potential for high reward. High risk investments are not a one way street however. With the potential for great reward, there is also potential for great loss. Conversely, there are investments that are on the lower end of the risk spectrum. They do not have inherently high risk, so they do not have the potential for great reward or great loss.

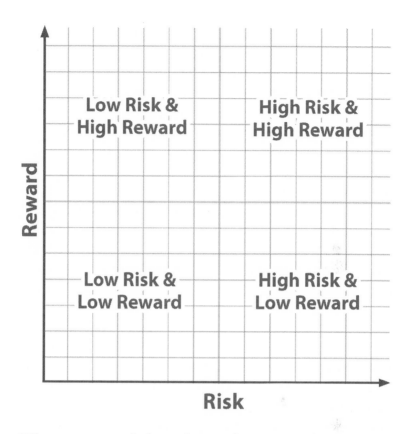

When most people hear the word *investing*, the first thing that comes to mind is the stock market. It's a good association, but it's also a limited one. It's like asking someone to name the first thing that comes to mind when you mention laundry detergent, and they answer, "Tide." We all know that this is a limited sort of response, because it's common knowledge that there are many types of laundry detergent on the market. But few people are aware that there are many ways to invest your money.

Investing through the stock market allows you to access what are commonly known as equity investments. You are purchasing ownership shares in a business when you invest in the stock market. The other commonly known market is the bond market, where one can invest in the fixed-income bonds that are issued by companies, municipalities, and governments. There are also markets that allow you to trade in commodities, such as gold, wheat, beef, etc. You can even invest in currencies from around the world. The wide range of possible Investments also includes real estate, ownership in limited partnerships, or a closely held business.

Basically, you are investing when you use your money in a way that you believe will give you a higher return at some point in the future. There are people who invest in sneakers. Some people invest in works of art. The basic thought process is this: "If I invest this money into this item or account or venture, I expect that my money will grow."

Many people are familiar with investing through actually owning a stock or mutual fund themselves. Their first encounter with the world of investing may have come either from a family member owning a stock or a bond, or through real estate that was owned in their family, or by being exposed to investing through a family-owned business. Whatever its origin, their experience with investing and investment management may not have been extensive.

The financial focus for most people is occupied by getting a good job, buying a home, buying a car, and making sure the kids can make it to college. For this reason, the world of investing to most people is as foreign as another language. And learning about the world of investing is about as much fun as learning that other language. That's why people turn to financial advisors or investment specialists to assist them with managing their investments.

Our changing economy and the longevity of the American population is making Step 4: Investing Wisely a very important issue in our lives. Earlier, I discussed the fact that more and more corporations are eliminating pension plans for their retirees. That fact, combined with the trend of people living a lot longer today than earlier generations did, means that the responsibility for funding retirement lands squarely on the shoulders of the individual employee.

If you have to fund and manage a nest egg that must last for decades once you retire, there's a strong possibility that you'll need to do a lot of financial planning to invest your money wisely. No institutional corporation is going to do it for you. Some folks have recently dubbed retirement planning as a YOYO plan, YOYO meaning "You're On Your Own".

Many people can go through Steps 1, 2 and 3 with relative ease. Planning Accordingly, Spending Cautiously, and Saving Diligently are well within the control of someone who is motivated to reach their financial goals. But Step 4: Invest Wisely can be very complex, and may require you to find a trusted advisor. Leaning on the experience of someone \who has extensive knowledge of how to invest will help you to Invest Wisely. This person should help you see the implications of how your investments will affect your overall financial position and subsequent financial goals.

STEP 5. GIFT GENEROUSLY

I've come to a simple conclusion when it comes to gifting. There are three kinds of people in this world:

1) Those who give to get

2) Those who get to give

3) Those who give to give

You may be familiar with these types of people. There are some folks who will give you something, expecting something in return. There are those who will only give a gift if someone gave them something first. Then there are those people who give for the sake of giving. They give because they can. They don't expect anything back and they don't need to get anything first to make them give. These are the people that make the world go around. They are selfless. They are aware of the fact that in the grand scheme of life we all need something and we all can give something. These people allow the natural flow of nature to occur and they benefit from it.

If you have the chance to read "The Go-Giver: A Little Story About a Powerful Business Idea" by Bob Burg and John David Mann, you will have a better understanding of the power of giving. The book tells a great story about how giving creates a powerful cycle in our lives. The power of giving permeates our personal lives, work lives, and social circles. By keeping the mindset of "giving to give," you can accomplish great things with both the expected and unexpected help of others.

From a financial planning perspective, Step 5: Gifting Generously can have a substantial impact on your path to financial success. I have placed gifting as the last step, but that doesn't mean it cannot be done earlier in the process. Many people have a disciplined approach to spending, saving and gifting. They either pay a 10% tithe to their church or provide some gift to an organization or family member.

I placed Gifting Generously as the last step because it is easier to gift *generously* when you have amassed sufficient assets to maintain your own lifestyle. Remember, the financial planning process is a lengthy journey, a path that is created every day by good and not so good financial choices. If you don't plan accordingly, spend cautiously, save diligently, and invest wisely, there's a strong possibility you won't have much to give to family or friends when you're alive or when you die.

One of the most memorable seminars I attended in my days working as a wholesaler included a powerful gifting story that I often share with my clients. One of the seminar speakers was talking about the power of financial planning, and how steps that are taken today can impact a family for generations to come. He asked this question: "Who in here, by a show of hands, can tell me the name of their great, great, great, great grandfather?" The reaction was not surprising. No one raised their hand. Then he made the following statement: "The Rockefellers can, the Carnegies can, the DuPonts can, the Mellons can. Why? Because each year they all get a payment from a family trust that was established years ago in the names of those deceased relatives."

Now, this may or may not be true, but these families certainly were some of the wealthiest families of their generation. And there is no doubt that the wealth that was created generations ago still benefits the decedents of these wealthy families to this day. The point the speaker was making was enormous: If you plan correctly, you can pass on wealth for generations to come. It may not make it to your great, great, great, great grandchild. But the gifting plans and strategies that you implement while alive can have a substantial impact on the lives of your children's children. In fact, your legacy —if planned for correctly— can affect more people than you ever thought possible.

People define financial success in many ways. For some, financial success means that they were able to accomplish a goal or achieve a level in life that their parents could not. For others, financial success means being able to maintain their lifestyle without being a burden on their children. Then there are those who believe that financial success is being able to leave something behind for generations to come.

No matter what the definition of success is, gifting is an integral part of the financial planning process. Many call this legacy planning. Those who have amassed any amount of wealth over their lifetime will eventually be gifting the assets to someone or some organization when they die. Many begin the gifting process early in their lives by gifting to children and family members. Others set up trusts that will dictate who gets what during their life and after their death.

Gifting generously during one's life and at death is a way of fulfilling the cycle of life. Wealth is a relative term. There will always be those who have more and those who will have less. By giving to those in need or organizations that support the needs of the less fortunate, you are contributing to the flowing stream of good will.

And giving doesn't always mean giving money. You can give food, assets, and even time. Giving generously—and more importantly, giving to give— is the last step to financial success. Once you have attained success, you then have the choice to help others along their path to financial success.

I have been in a fortunate position in my line of business as a financial advisor, as it has afforded me the opportunity to work with people who have walked various financial paths. I have worked with people in their early 20's just starting off their careers, and with people in their 30's and 40's busy starting up families and businesses. And I've worked with people in their 50's and 60's who are focusing on entering retirement.

The best insight however, comes from those in the twilight stages of their lives. These people have travelled a long path, and have some great stories about the financial choices they've made that have led them to meeting with me. These people have worked very hard for many years, and have been able to amass a small fortune. They were not born with silver spoons in their mouths. They were not heirs to large amounts of wealth. They simply followed, in their own way, the 5 Steps to Financial Success.

As I uncovered the stories of these financially successful people in the twilight of their lives, I would hear a common theme. These people learned from an early stage in life that they had to develop a healthy mutual relationship with their money. They followed the K L T / C P R rules regarding their money. They knew it, they liked it and they trusted it. Then they learned to communicate, be productive, and respect their money. They learned to live beneath their means.

For some, it wasn't an option. Because they were not wealthy to begin with and had few financial options, every dollar earned went to fund their basic life necessities. There wasn't a rampant credit card industry that was giving out loans whether you were qualified or not. Everything was paid for with cash. They bought what they needed and they needed what they bought. These people realized that they had to rely on themselves to make ends meet, and that they had to provide for their own rainy day fund. So saving wasn't a luxury, it was a necessity.

As the years went by, these people would one day take a closer look at their savings accounts, and realize that they needed to do something to make their money grow. More importantly, they realized that they now had options to do other things with their saved assets. They could buy a home, purchase a business, invest in the stock market, or invest in some other venture that would provide a return higher than what a savings account did. There was little or no debt to service, so their cash flow went toward the basic living expenses, a mortgage, and some other savings and investments.

Before they knew it, the combination of spending cautiously, saving diligently, increasing salaries, the power of compounding interest, and capital appreciation had made these people millionaires! They had amassed a large enough estate to provide them income to maintain their lifestyle in retirement. As they moved on in life, they were faced with finding tax-efficient ways to give assets to family members and to organizations that held a special place in their lives. I have been blessed and fortunate to be the person in their lives to hear their story and to help them with their financial planning.

Now I have to admit, not all of the stories I've heard over my years as a financial advisor are so nicely tied together and close with a warm and happy ending. I have worked with many people who are entering the twilight phase of their lives petrified by the unknown. These people don't have enough saved, they continuously overspend, they don't know what options they have, and they need help. The sad truth for these people is that you can't relive the life that has passed.

The common thread in these people's lives is that they didn't follow the 5 Steps to Financial Success. They wish that they could go back in time and set up a financial plan. They wish they could go back in time and spend their money better. They all wish that they could have started saving more for retirement earlier in their lives. But it can't be done. Some of the hardest meetings I have had in my career centered around telling someone who has worked all his life that I cannot help him reach his goal because he has neither the time nor the money to get there.

MOTIVATIONAL THOUGHTS/NOTES:

MOTIVATE *Your* **MONEY!**

Plan > Spend > Save > Invest > Gift

CHAPTER 4

The Power of Planning

*Planning without action
is futile, action without
planning is fatal.*

— UNKNOWN

Billionaire John D. Rockefeller introduced his 5 children to planning when they were still at an early age Each received an allowance of 25 cents per week, plus they had the opportunity to earn additional money by growing vegetables or raising animals. He also required each of his five sons to record their expenses. They had control over their money, though they were asked to give 10 percent of their earnings to charity and to save 10 percent.

We all try to instill good habits in our children. Rockefeller knew that in order for his estate to last for generations, his children and their children had to understand how to control their money. He knew that they would inherit the ability to make financial choices that would either perpetuate the wealth or destroy the estate that was built during his lifetime. Today, generations later, the legacy and wealth of the Rockefeller family live on.

Most of us are not born into the massive amounts of wealth enjoyed by the Rockefeller family. But that doesn't mean planning for the financial future is any less important for us than for them. In the most fundamental sense, planning is the key to financial success. You will also need determination, persistence, and knowledge as you go along your path. However, all these elements provide little help if there isn't a financial game plan that is followed throughout your lifetime.

One of the main challenges to successful financial planning is balance. By balance, I mean prioritizing the right assets and making the right financial decisions to maintain the ever-changing needs, wants, and wishes that exist in our lives. As we move through the various phases of the financial planning life cycle, the needs, wants, and wishes of our lives will surely change. But in order to strike the right financial balance in life, there needs to be a proper hierarchy that drives financial goals. How often do you sit down and ask yourself: What is a need? What is a want? And what is a wish? And more importantly, how do they all affect your personal financial plan and overall financial process?

Financial needs, wants, and wishes can be the driving forces behind a successful plan. However, if there is no clarity, no hierarchy, and no sense of urgency to the needs, wants and wishes in your life, that is a recipe for financial disaster. I usually associate the three components with a three-tiered pyramid. I have called it a personal "Goal Pyramid." The base of the pyramid houses the needs, the middle section makes up the wants, and the top of the pyramid would be wishes.

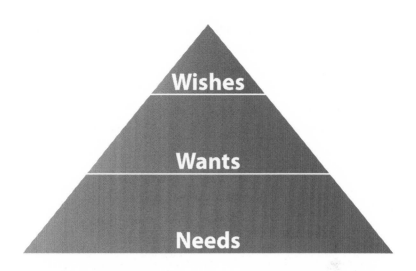

Needs could be viewed as things that are needed to maintain one's life. Food, shelter, clothing, and other such necessities make up the base of the pyramid. Wants could be viewed as a new car, a nice evening out, or a new gadget. Wishes could be viewed as a dream vacation, a new boat, or a vacation home. Most of us finance our short term and mid-term needs with cash flow from either our jobs or business. We set up a budget to include groceries, car payment, mortgage, rent, etc. We may also have cash saved up in an account for a rainy day. And some may have investment accounts that were established for short term and mid-term "needs".

As we move up the pyramid we see that there are "wants" in our lives that require planning, too. That family vacation will require some planning to make sure that there's enough saved up. Disney cruises are a lot of fun, but they aren't cheap! At the top of the pyramid we have "wishes" such as, for example, that vacation home you've always dreamed about. These types of goals, though lofty, are not out of reach.

If the proper planning is implemented from an early stage, it is very possible to make it to the top of your "Goal Pyramid." It does take a lot of work, a lot of time, a lot of discipline, and a lot of energy, but most importantly, it takes the proper motivation to get on that financial path and stay there. And it's just as important to know that it doesn't take a lot of money to reach your goals. It just takes the right plan, good financial decisions, and time.

A goal without a plan is just a wish. No matter if you're planning for short term or long term needs, you need to have a financial plan in place to achieve success and have any chance of reaching a financial goal. The same can be said for wants and wishes. Generally, people have a financial game plan in place to ensure that their short term life needs are being satisfied. Long term planning for needs, wants and wishes takes more time and energy. Because of the time, energy, and dedication needed to maintain longer term financial plans, many people either fail to plan properly or don't plan at all.

A great example of the lack of long term planning for a financial need is the sad state of retirement savings in America. We can also consider the fact that many American families are woefully underinsured. These current situations in America are a direct result of a lack of financial planning for long term needs, which must be addressed before we can move up the Goal Pyramid to address other goals. Many people's Goals Pyramid is built on a shaky base. And if the base of the pyramid is weak, the chance of building a successful financial plan is slim to none.

So what can you do to better your odds of reaching financial success? The first step is to view your needs, wants, and wishes as both short term and long term goals. What needs- based goals do you want to accomplish today, next week, next year? And then, what types of long term and short term wants and wishes are linked to your goals?

As I just mentioned, motivating yourself and motivating your money are essential to reaching your financial goals. Getting to those goals requires planning and SMART goal setting. You may be familiar with the SMART acronym. It is often used to describe the key elements needed for successful goal setting and planning: the goal and plan must be Specific, Measurable, Accurate, Realistic, and Timely. I have found that utilizing the SMART method for goal setting helps to motivate people when setting financial goals. Let's take a look at how it works:

Your specific financial goal may be saving for a family vacation. You'll need to know how much the vacation costs and how much you can save. These are the measurable components of the goal. Once the cost of the vacation is determined, an accurate savings strategy must be implemented and monitored. The vacation goal must be a realistic goal that can be achieved in a timely manner. A four-month sailing trip through the Caribbean on a 50- foot yacht might be a dream vacation, but how realistic is it and how long would it take you to save for it?

Practicing the SMART goal setting process can help you on your path to financial success. By applying these SMART criteria to short term, mid-term, and long term goals, you will develop a healthy habit of using your money efficiently. By starting this process early in life, you will have the ability to build a strong financial foundation that will support you and your family for years to come.

From a financial planning perspective, many planners agree that there are 4 fundamental financial planning life phases:

If we were to follow the typical American, we would see a financial life phase that looks like this:

Let's give our example a name. We'll call her Jen. Jen is in high school and decides to work part time to pay for a car and help alleviate the family's auto insurance expenses (isn't that nice of her!). With the first dollar she earned, Jen has entered the financial life cycle merry go round. Jen now has the ability to turn her time, energy and resources into an income stream. She also has the ability to affect her economy from both a micro and a macro level. She will now have the ability to take the 5 steps to financial success. She will have the choice to plan accordingly, spend cautiously, save diligently, invest wisely and gift generously.

One of the first steps that Jen must face, now that she is in the Asset Accumulation phase, is to structure a budget. It's very hard to accumulate assets if you spend everything you earn. The budget serves as the blueprint for every successful financial plan.

In her budget, Jen will determine how much she earns after taxes, also known as her net income. If her job provides her with a company-sponsored retirement plan, she will have an easy way to start a diligent savings strategy. Her contributions to her retirement plan will come out of her paycheck automatically. These contributions will also help her to lower her taxes, since they are before-tax contributions. Because she's still a minor, she probably won't have to deal with insurance deductions. She'll have the joy of dealing with those fun options later in life.

So Jen now has an idea of what her net income is. She also knows what her car payments and insurance premiums will be, and the cost of living the life of a teenager. So, even at this early stage of life there are major life and/or financial obligations. But that doesn't prevent Jen from taking some significant steps at an early age — steps that can have a profound effect on her financial future. If she were to decide, for example, to take a portion of her paycheck and invest it in an S&P 500 index fund or ETF, (Exchange-traded fund), she would be able to take advantage of one of the biggest determining factors in successful investing: time.

Although at this stage in life Jen doesn't have the large amounts of capital needed to invest, she does have the option in invest in vehicles called DRIPs. DRIP stands for "dividend reinvestment plan, which offers Jan the opportunity to invest small amounts in a particular stock over time. Instead of being distributed, the dividends earned will be used to purchase more shares along with her systematic contributions to the plan.

As we have seen, there are many options available to someone as young as Jen that will allow her to have an early head start in the asset accumulation phase. Her contributions to her retirement plan, a systematic savings strategy and an early investment plan will allow her to move on to college or the work force with some highly productive and beneficial financial habits.

Jen is now in college. With the work bug in her from an early age still thriving, she continues to balance school and work. She may be working because she wants to, or because she has to. She may have to take out loans or she may be fortunate enough to have parents or grandparents assist her in financing her college experience. In either situation, Jan still has to make financial choices every day that will affect her ability to reach her financial goals.

One of the biggest challenges that will face Jen in her college years is the ability and ease of obtaining credit. Banks are very aware that colleges are the breeding grounds of financially successful people. They know that once Jen finishes her time in college, she will probably have the potential to earn greater income. If they can get ahold of Jen and provide her a line of credit early in her life, they can make a lot of money off this one woman—but only if Jen misuses her ability to utilize debt. However, because Jen has started and maintained a disciplined approach to managing her finances, she won't fall into the credit card debt trap.

Jen is now 22 years old and about to graduate with an engineering degree. She's got a few employment offers lined up and is weighing her options. Salary, benefits, and growth potential are all deciding factors in what will be her first significant opportunity to accumulate assets. She decides on a national firm, and her career in engineering begins in earnest.

Life moves on for Jan, and she realizes that she wants to own a home. She's 26, has been working for a few years, and realizes that the capital that's been going toward rent could be used to invest in an asset that she can own and post entail rent out herself. Because she's been saving and investing since she was 16, Jen has been able to amass enough capital to make a substantial down payment on her new townhome.

This sizeable chunk of money will help her to get a better rate on her home loan than if her down payment was lower, and will make her loan payments more manageable. Because of the financial choices she made and the planning steps she implemented over a span of just 10 years, Jen is already realizing an American dream: homeownership.

As Jen is out shopping one day for that just-right piece of art for her new home (she only pays with cash by the way, via her checkcard) she meets Ben, a young up-and- coming attorney. He's 30, and is following a similar financial path to Jen. Ben owns his home, earns a good income and is looking to start his own firm. Jen and Ben decide to start down a life path together and in a few years they decide to get married.

Now the financial planning fun really begins. Both Jen and Ben own a home. Do they sell one, none, or both? If they do sell, what should they do with the proceeds of the sale? If they keep one, what are the consequences of renting the property? Let's say they decide to sell both of their smaller homes, and use the proceeds to purchase a bigger home that would be just right for a starting family.

A few years go by. Jen and Ben have continued to work hard. They plan accordingly, spend cautiously, and save diligently. When they welcome their first child, they decide that they could use the help of a certified financial planner to help smooth their way on their lifelong financial journey. After all, managing investments, insurance, taxes, retirement plans, and estate plans at the same time can be an arduous task for even the most ambitious individual.

As Jen and Ben move through their high-income-earning years, they continue to accumulate assets. Their 401(k) plans grow and their stock and bond portfolios go up and down. They purchase rental real estate. Jen becomes a managing director of her engineering firm. Ben opens his own firm and becomes the owner of a successful, growing practice.

They will continue to accumulate assets; however, their focus begins to shift toward asset preservation. With young children and a business that generates significant income, Jen and Ben need to make sure that a plan is in place that will allow for their family's continued financial success should any serious injury or premature death befall either or both parents.

Jen and Ben are now in their 50's and in their peak earning years. Their 3 children have made it through college, so

Ben and Jen are now looking seriously at how their lives will play out in retirement. They set a retirement date and optimistically shoot for retirement in their mid-to late- 60's. This phase will be characterized as distributions through life.

Retirement distribution planning is vastly more complicated when compared to retirement accumulation planning. For the many years that Jen and Ben were focusing on asset growth and protection, the financial goal was to secure a nest egg that could be transitioned into an income stream once they retired. Growing an investment portfolio and a retirement plan took time. They could dollar cost average by making systematic purchases over time. They could use their real estate assets for both capital appreciation and income generation. There are many options.

The distribution phase, by contrast, is tricky because you still have to manage your assets to make them grow. Retirement can last a long time for Jen and Ben. Now they have to add the extra factor of turning the assets earmarked for retirement into a tax-efficient income stream that will last the lifetime of two people. Which accounts do they spend first? What financial vehicles are available to turn assets into a lifetime income stream? Will there be anything left for the next generation? The list of questions can go on.

Jen and Ben have practiced some healthy financial habits for most of their lives. They have made good financial decisions over their lifetime that allowed them to grow their personal financial fortune into a significant estate. Their children now have grandchildren, and they have been fortunate to impart their seeds of financial knowledge to their heirs and can watch their family's financial forest grow.

Statistically, Ben will die before Jen. If Ben dies first, Jen will then embark on the last phase of personal financial planning: distributing assets upon death, a phase that is wrought with emotion and can be extremely costly if not planned for correctly. Many people are aware of income taxes, fewer are aware of investment taxes, even fewer are familiar with estate taxes.

Estate tax, or death tax as some call it, can have a significant effect on legacy planning. If Jen and Ben have a substantial estate valued over certain dollar limits and fail to plan correctly, they may be exposing their heirs to a large tax bill on the assets they inherit. Having an up to date will, trust documents, and properly titled assets are some of the key steps that can be taken to properly plan for the distribution of assets upon death. If these key steps are done correctly, Jen and Ben can strategically pass on their hard earned assets in a cost effective and tax efficient manner.

Granted, the Jen and Ben story is oversimplified. However, that doesn't mean that this situation is either far-fetched or unreal. There are many people who have lived the life and experienced the scenarios I described in the Jen and Ben story. I know this because I've worked with people like Jen and Ben on a daily basis. I've worked with people who are living through every phase of the personal financial planning cycle. Those who have made it through the process successfully have all practiced healthy financial habits. Starting from a young age, they made good financial choices, consistently following the 5 Steps to Financial Success. There is no mystery to their success, nor was there any get-rich-quick scheme. They succeeded because they understood the power of planning, and realized that the power of planning, combined with healthy financial habits and wise financial choices, equals long term financial success.

As you take a look at your current personal financial situation, you are likely asking yourself what are the main concerns you should have as you move through the phases of the financial planning process. Every person's financial plan and financial motivation are as unique as their fingerprints. However, there are some universally accepted challenges and concerns associated with each phase of the financial planning process. There are also consistent factors that are involved throughout the entire cycle.

Below are some examples of what the typical person would focus on while they are moving through the personal financial planning cycle:

ASSET ACCUMULATION PHASE:

- Maintain a realistic and sustainable budget.

- Develop a systematic savings strategy.

- Look for ways to save, in both a tax advantaged account and a taxable account. This can be achieved by either funding a company-sponsored retirement plan, IRA, Roth IRA, savings account, money market account, or a mutual fund.

- Try to minimize the use of credit card debt.

- Establish short term, mid-term and long term savings strategies by setting up specific accounts for each goal. Consider opening a money market account or establishing a CD for goals that need to be achieved in less than 3 years. For goals that you aim at achieving in 3 to 7 years, consider using investment vehicles that do not have a lot of historical volatility, such as fixed income investments. For longer term goals, it can be beneficial to use equity type investments if your time horizon is over 10 years. Having a balance of assets in your portfolio that aligns with your tolerance for risk will be key to mid-term and long term investing.

- When purchasing a home, be aware of how to use debt. Mortgages are used by most people who either do not have sufficient capital to buy a home or would rather use leverage as a means to purchase the asset. Loan to value and credit scores are key components to mortgages. If you can keep your loan to value below 80% and you have above average credit scores, you can negotiate for the best interest rates.

- The journey toward a comfortable retirement begins early in the Asset Accumulation phase. Take advantage of company sponsored retirement plans such as 401(k), 403(b) 457 plans. If your company provides a match, contribute at least an amount that gets you the full match. It's free money! Tax advantaged accounts provide what is called triple compounding of your interest: 1) Your principal earns interest, 2) Your interest earns interest, 3) The money you would have paid taxes on earns interest.

- As you continue to grow investable assets, be aware of the tax ramifications of your investments. Purchasing a stock, bond, mutual fund or ETF does not create a taxable event. However, be aware that some stocks produce dividends. These can be taxable. Most bonds provide either a taxable or tax free interest. Mutual funds can distribute capital gains and interest even if you don't sell the shares. ETF's can also distribute dividends and income. Work with a financial planner or CPA to get a better understanding of how your investments are taxed.

- Real estate and other non-correlated investment assets can serve to diversify an investment portfolio. These areas of investing can be highly profitable; however, due to their complexity, it's best to find a resource that specializes in the area you want to invest in.

- If you own a business, there are more variables to deal with. You have both your personal financial plan as well as your business financial plan. Keeping the two separate will be the biggest challenge. I have dedicated a chapter to business owners that will cover more information.

ASSET PRESERVATION PHASE:

- As financial assets grow there will be a need to protect and preserve these assets.

- The most common tool used to help protect and preserve assets is insurance.

- Home and auto insurance are required in most states. As these are critical financial assets, it is important to make sure that proper and adequate coverage is maintained.

- Life insurance is a tool that can be used to replace potential future income or provide capital in case of unexpected death. Explore employer sponsored life insurance as well as individual policies.

- Disability insurance can help to replace income in case of partial or full disability.

- Health insurance can help to offset medical expenses. Consider various policy types such as HMO and PPO.

- Long term care insurance can provide income for maintaining one's lifestyle if their health deteriorates due to old age.

- All insurance costs money. The main idea behind insurance is that you'd rather have it and not need it— instead of needing it and not having it.

DISTRIBUTION DURING LIFE:

- The most familiar concept associated with this phase is retirement.

- It is important to know that during the distribution phase there is still a need for asset accumulation and asset protection strategies.

- There are 4 key challenges in the distribution phase: Taxes, Inflation, Market Volatility, and Longevity.

- Tax management is a constant throughout every phase of personal financial planning. Producing a tax-efficient income stream from various investment vehicles requires constant planning.

- Inflation or erosion of purchase power can erode a distribution plan. If assets are not keeping up with inflation, your assets will be depleted too quickly in your attempt to finance a retirement lifestyle.

- Market volatility deals with the timing of stock market decreases and how that can affect a distribution plan.

- Longevity risk is one of the biggest concerns for those in the distribution phase. Life expectancy continues to increase. How do you ensure that your money will last as long as you do? No one wants their money to retire before they expire.

- Health care cost is a growing concern for many retirees. Medicare may not provide sufficient coverage. Medicare supplement plans may be needed and can be costly.

- Gifting is another way to distribute assets during life. This is a good way to reduce the value of the estate, and possibly reduce estate taxes.

DISTRIBUTION AT DEATH:

- The probate process is the system by which the assets of a deceased person are distributed to heirs. It can be a complicated process that is open to the public.

- A will provides guidance and describes the wishes of the deceased. A will doesn't avoid the probate process.

- Choosing an executor in your will is essential.

- Not having a will is considered "dying intestate." This takes a lot of distribution choices out of the hands of heirs and puts them in the hands of the resident state regulations.

- Accounts or contracts that have a designated beneficiary or pass via contract law can be used to avoid probate. These can be IRAs, 401(k), annuities and life insurance. Upon the death of the account owner, the beneficiary is immediately entitled to the asset.

- Accounts titled as "Joint with rights of survivorship" or "Transfer on Death" can also avoid probate.

- Trusts can be used as a means to avoid probate and fulfill the wishes of the deceased.

- Life insurance death benefits are payable directly to beneficiaries. The payments are normally income tax free.

- Annuity contracts are also paid directly to beneficiaries. Only the growth of an after tax annuity is taxable to the beneficiary. If an annuity is funded with before-tax assets (IRA, 401(k) etc.), all distributions are fully taxable.

- Investment assets such as stocks, bonds, mutual funds, and real estate are given a "step up in basis" which is the value of the asset on the date of death of the owner. This is the new cost basis of the asset for the person that inherits the asset.

As you can see from the numerous points above, there are a lot of financial planning considerations that may have to be addressed during one's lifetime. Not everyone will have to contend with every point, but a majority of people will have to deal with most of these challenges as they move through the financial planning cycle.

"Your emotions should be colorful. Your finances should be black and white."
- MAC GARDNER

MOTIVATIONAL THOUGHTS/NOTES:

MOTIVATE Your **MONEY!**

Plan > Spend > Save > Invest > Gift

CHAPTER 5

The Five Point Wealth Management Plan

Planning is bringing the future into the present so that you can do something about it now.

—ALAN LAKEIN

The purpose of this section of the book is not to make you a professional financial planner. There are many people who have made personal financial planning their profession. There is a Certified Financial Planner designation that can be attained after satisfying a very rigorous set of requirements. These people know enough about financial planning to be deadly. I want you to leave this chapter with enough information to make you dangerous. That is, I want you to know the basics about each wealth management area that will help you to be knowledgeable and aware for any meeting you may have with a financial planning professional.

As you move through the financial planning lifecycle, you will realize that some planning areas will have a greater emphasis over others. The 5 Point Wealth Management Plan can be used in conjunction with your financial cycle to provide a tailored and goal-specific financial guideline.

Most financial decisions over your lifetime will fit into one of the 5 points. If you can address all 5 of these points as you travel through your financial life journey, it will be easier to reach your financial goals and achieve financial success.

As you read about the 5 point wealth management plan, it is important to keep in mind that I use the term "wealth management" and not "financial management." The strategies and concepts that will be discussed in this chapter are used by those who view their financial worth as wealth. Wealth is a relative term. You don't have to be rich to have wealth. You do, however, need to have a mindset built on your strong belief that you can create, gain, maintain, and retain wealth. Those who have worked to achieve financial success are acutely aware of their power to influence their financial future. They don't view their finances as an inanimate object, but rather as a creative and productive force that can be used to reach goals that formerly they could only dream of.

Use the 5 point wealth management plan to help you motivate your money. Use it to give your wealth guidance, help your wealth be more productive, and reach your lifelong financial goals.

The best analogy I can give that describes how the various concepts of Motivate Your Money work together is to compare them with a car. "Understanding the 3 F's" is the engine to every person's financial car. Your family, finances, and future create the financial goals and create the motivation to achieve financial success. The "5 Steps to Financial Success" serve as your car's steering wheel. The decisions that lead to whether you turn right, left or go straight are similar to the daily choices that you make with your money. Do you plan, spend, save, invest and gift?

The "Financial Lifecycle" works as your car's GPS. By knowing where you are and where you want to be it is easier to reach your destination. The "5 Point Wealth Management Plan" serves as the wheels of your car. These 5 areas of wealth management and the inherent strategies and tactics involved allow your financial engine, steering wheel, and GPS to successfully work together and drive you toward your goals. The 5 Point Wealth Management Plan is the financial rubber that meets your personal financial planning road.

If you're wondering what fuels your financial engine, you need to understand how all of these concepts work together. A client once asked me that question and I shared this analogy. That was his "aha moment." I looked at him and smiled. He knew the answer. The fuel that makes your financial engine run smoothly is the whole set of daily choices you make with your money. Good financial choices are like high octane fuel, bad choices are like adding diesel fuel to a gas engine.

INVESTMENT MANAGEMENT

Of all of the 5 points of the Wealth Management Plan, investments is the "sexiest." This could be due to our society's perception of Wall Street, or perhaps due to all of the media coverage that the world of investments receives. Whatever the reason, investments and investment management are integral factors in the financial planning process.

Fundamentally, an investment is a financial transaction that involves risk. This is not limited to investing in the stock market. One could argue that any time you use your money with an expectation of getting some sort of short term or long term return, it can be considered an investment. This should not be confused with gambling, as I mentioned and explained earlier. Neither should it be confused with saving, which should involve little to no risk.

People can invest in many ways. Besides stocks and bonds, you can invest in real assets such as gold, real estate, timber, artwork, wine, shoes, currency, gemstones, furniture; the list can go on for quite a while. There are also ways to invest in market volatility by purchasing options or derivatives. Then there's investing in a business. If you own a business, every dollar that goes into that business is an investment in the growth and expected success of that business.

The fundamental premise of investing is the concept of risk versus reward. This premise suggests that the more risk an investment contains, the higher the expected reward. Conversely, the less inherent risk, the less potential growth. In either situation there can also be a relative degree of loss of your investment.

Because risk is such an integral part of investing, it is imperative that an asset allocation based on an individual's current risk tolerance is established. Even more important is making sure that risk tolerance and portfolio allocation are consistently in line over a long period of time.

Determining risk tolerance can be accomplished by looking at a few factors. Time is a significant factor. How long do you want to invest, or when will you need the asset? Market volatility is another factor. How much up and down of the market can you stomach? Another important question is: what do you need the asset to do for you? All of these questions must be taken into consideration to determine risk tolerance.

Investment tools for short and mid-term goals can include various after-tax accounts. Brokerage accounts, mutual funds, and other investment vehicles are popular options that allow you to participate in the investment arena. Stocks and bonds can be bought and sold through a broker dealer. Mutual funds can be purchased and sold through the fund directly or through a broker.

The world of stock and bond market investing has changed significantly over the last few decades. The ability and cost of owning equities and fixed income investments has become easier and cheaper. In the 1960's, most people who were interested in buying stocks did so through a stock broker, who picked up the phone and sold you stock for a sizeable commission.

Then in the 1970's, the actively-managed mutual fund became popular. A mutual fund allows you to own a "basket" comprising a variety of investments. This can provide diversification and spread investment risk. Early mutual funds carried some high management fees, but as the mutual fund industry evolved, costs began to decrease.

In the 1990's, Exchange Traded Funds were created as another investment alternative. ETF's are cost effective and trade like stocks. They follow an index and can be used to create a diversified investment portfolio. Deciding whether to own an individual stock, a bond, a mutual fund or an ETF depends on the investment parameters of the individual. Each investment vehicle has its benefits and its detriment.

Another popular investment vehicle is real estate, which can be owned in the form of a personal residence, commercial property, or raw land. You can also own real estate through partnerships or through trusts known as Real Estate Investment Trusts (REITs), which invest in real estate investments. Specific rules apply to these investments and demand that assets must be distributed annually.

Commodity investments include gold, precious metals, grain, livestock, oil, etc. Commodities trade like stocks and bonds on a market. They are non-correlated investments; that is, they don't move like the stock market. Some investors use commodities in their investment portfolio as a way to diversify their holdings.

Many believe that when constructing an optimal investment portfolio, you should own a mix of assets that provide varying types of investment results. Some of the assets can provide capital appreciation, some can provide income, and some will do both. An investor interested in building a portfolio of US companies can choose from many companies of varying sizes that can be owned. Such companies are described by their market capitalization size. Capitalization is the value of the amount of outstanding shares of a publicly traded company. Small cap companies have a market capitalization of under $2 billion, mid cap companies have a value between $2 and $10 billion, and large cap companies have values over $10 billion.

Companies that are at different stages of their life cycle have differing historical growth patterns. Small and mid-sized companies have a lot more potential for long term growth compared to large companies that have already experienced their growth phase. Large companies tend to focus on providing dividends to their shareholders. Small and midsize companies, however, are more likely to put their growth back into their business as opposed to paying out dividends. By owning shares of various sized companies, your portfolio can benefit from gaining various ranges of capital growth and potential dividends.

The development of a global economy has allowed for investment in international companies and international economies. Historically, international investments have provided another diversification option for American investors. Although the international market has experienced a lot of relative volatility compared to the US market, there is plenty of opportunity for capital growth and income outside of the United States. Having some exposure to international investments can serve as another long term investment resource that can help your portfolio grow.

Fixed income investments such as treasury bonds, corporate bonds, and municipal bonds are good investment options for those primarily seeking income from their investment. Historically, bonds are not as volatile as stocks. Whereas stocks were created to provide ownership shares in a company, bonds were created to provide a fixed and determinable financing source for businesses looking to raise capital. Bond investments provide a yield, which is essentially the cost a company pays to borrow your money.

Historically, long term bonds pay a higher yield but they are more susceptible to market volatility. Short term bonds pay a lower yield but they are not as volatile. Though bonds may not fluctuate as much as stocks, it is important to know that they are nevertheless investments, and there is risk involved in owning bonds. A company can go out of business or can be mismanaged. This can affect the value of the bond. Moreover, bonds are affected by changes in interest rates. When interest rates go up, bond values may go down. And vice-versa: when interest rates go down, bond values can increase.

When I sit with clients to discuss investments, they usually have a lot of questions and voice quite a few opinions. Many falsely believe that investments are a one-sided coin, so that once they invest, they can expect continued sustainable growth year over year. Some believe that double-digit portfolio growth is the norm. Many forget about the stock market crashes that occurred in 1987 (Black Monday), 2001 (Dot Com Bubble), and in 2008 (The Great Recession).

Though historically stocks have the potential for capital growth, one can't expect that growth to happen every year. One of the expectations I try to convey to clients is that investing essentially deals with risk. Risk just can't be eliminated when you're dealing with investing. However, it can be mitigated. You mitigate risk by owning certain types of investments. Many in the financial services industry call this "asset allocation." If we have a historical understanding of the levels of risk inherent in the different types of investments, we can create a portfolio that follows the expectations of our tolerance for risk.

Rule of 100

A popular question that many clients ask is: "What should my overall long term asset allocation be? How much should I have in stocks and how much should I have in bonds?" The answer to that question is determined by many factors in that person's life. Family goals, financial goals, time horizon, and appetite for risk are all contributors to that person's optimal asset allocation.

There are some concepts that have been developed by financial planners to provide a basic guideline for asset allocation. This guideline is called the "Rule of 100." In order to get an idea of how much stock and bond you should have in your portfolio, you start with the number 100, and then subtract your age. The resulting figure represents how much, as a percent, you should have in stocks. Here's an example of 3 individuals aged 25, 50, and 75:

> - *Portfolio of 25 year old: 100 - 25 = 75*
>   *(75% in stocks, 25% in bonds)*
>
> - *Portfolio of 50 year old: 100 - 50 = 50*
>   *(50% in stocks, 50% in bonds)*
>
> - *Portfolio of 75 year old: 100 - 75 = 25*
>   *(25% in stocks, 75% in bonds)*

If you noticed the trend that the older you get the more your portfolio should be invested in bonds, you're on the right path. The rationale behind the "Rule of 100" is that when an investor is younger, say 25, he has the advantage of time—both the time to invest in the stock market and the time to make up for market losses—before reaching retirement age. Because stocks provide a historically higher return versus bonds over the long term, a younger investor could gain the greatest benefit from a portfolio that is heavily invested in stocks and can therefore provide a better chance for long term growth.

As you get older a few things happen. First, your time horizon for using the money is closing. If you are 50 and plan on retiring at age 65, that gives you 15 years to invest before you begin to take distributions from the account. A lot can happen in 15 years, so it is important to have exposure to stocks.

However, if too much is exposed to stocks, you run the risk of having an account that is susceptible to stock market volatility. Think 1987, 2001, and 2008, when many people lost 50% of their assets due to stock market corrections. By having 50% of a portfolio in a more conservative investment at age 50, you are mitigating your stock market risk. This portion of your portfolio may not grow as much as much as your other investments, but you're not looking for it to grow a lot. You want it to grow a little and not lose a lot.

When you reach retirement and later stages in life, you should still have exposure to the stock market. Historically, that may be the best hedge against inflation. The main goal at this stage of life is to maintain the account and have some growth, while distributions are being made to finance retirement. Any major market swings during this phase of life can cause irreparable damage to an investment portfolio and can eliminate the possibility of having enough assets to maintain your lifestyle throughout your retirement.

For that reason, the fixed income portion of a retiree's portfolio should be fairly resistant to market volatility. By having a larger portion of the account invested in fixed income investments, there is a stronger probability that the asset will grow slowly and will not be as volatile as a portfolio that includes a large percentage of stocks.

I can remember a client meeting I had early in my career. This client had worked as an engineer for many years. He and his wife amassed a sizeable estate by following the rules I described early in this book. They were able to retire in their mid-50's. He provided me a nugget that I share with my clients regularly. He said he had learned from his dad the trick to investing, "Buy stocks to get rich, buy bonds to stay rich!" He wasn't all that wrong. If you can grow a retirement nest egg to a large enough size, and then convert that asset to a fixed income portfolio with less market volatility while creating a sustainable income stream, you've done a great job of self-insuring your retirement income.

Rule of 72

Another popular discussion that revolves around investments is the power of growth. Many people are lulled by the investment siren song titled "return on investment." They want to know:

- "How did the portfolio perform?"

- "What is the 1, 3, 5, and 10 year return?"

- "How did this investment perform versus its benchmark?"

These are all valid questions when taken in the right context. Performance and cost of any investment is something that should be monitored. But if expectations are to be met, they must be realistic. Many people believe that investments can provide astronomical returns. That's possible, but not very probable. And if it does happen, there's a very strong possibility that the market will correct itself. Every bubble eventually pops.

My favorite investment management "welcome to reality" rule is the Rule of 72. At one time or another, you may have asked yourself something like this: "If I invested $50,000 today, how long will it take me to double my money?" With the power of some financial planning and a calculator, I can give you an answer using the "Rule of 72." If you could earn a 10% return every year, you would double your money in approximately 7.2 years. Not bad huh? Now you've got to ask yourself, where can you find an investment that will assure you a 10% return every year?

The Rule of 72 works this way: You divide 72 by the rate of return. So, 72 divided by 10 equals 7.2. If we look at a more probable annual return of 5% we see that it will take approximately 14.4 years for your money to double (72 / 5 = 14.4). If you want to find out what rate of return you will need to double your money in a certain amount of years, we simply move the equation around to get the answer. An investment will need to earn 15% per year to double in 5 years. That's an easy and clear method to determine rates of returns and time frames, but it doesn't answer the important question: How do you get these kinds of returns? And more importantly, is it possible to get these returns consistently each and every year?

Qualified vs. Non-Qualified Accounts

Earlier, in the section on investing for the long term, I discussed the power of utilizing the growth potential of stocks and the income potential of bonds. Up to this point, we have been dealing with the actual investment vehicles. Now, we need to focus on another important aspect of investing: the *type of account* we utilize to save for our various financial goals. The terms Qualified and Nonqualified describe the IRS tax status of an investment account. Qualified means the assets "qualify" for special tax treatment. Non-qualified means the account does not.

The special tax treatments in qualified accounts can be very powerful tools for financing long term goals. Most company-sponsored retirement accounts fall under the status of a qualified account. Contributions to these accounts can be made on a pre-tax basis, which can help to lower your taxable income. Assets held in this type of account have the ability to grow on a tax-deferred basis. This may not sound like a glamorous feature, but tax deferred growth can provide some wonderfully astonishing long term results.

The power of tax deferred growth amplifies the theory of compounding interest. Albert Einstein is often quoted on this point. He said, "Compound interest is the eighth wonder of the world. He who understands it, earns it...he who doesn't, pays it." Compounding interest is the ability of money to earn money, and the subsequent long term exponential growth that results from saving and earning interest. If we were to compare compounding interest between a qualified account and a nonqualified account, we would see that the biggest difference is the effect of taxation on the two accounts.

Let's take the example of $100 in a savings account versus the same amount in a 401(k) plan. In the savings account your $100 earns 5% interest. After a year, you now have $105. As years go by you earn interest on the initial $100 and you earn interest on the interest. But because the $100 is in a nonqualified after-tax account, you have to pay taxes on the 5% interest you earned. So, depending on your tax bracket, your net growth may only be between 3% or 4%. You had to give some of the total growth back because of the type of account that held your $100.

Now let's take a look at how your $100 works in your 401(k). Because the contribution to the 401(k) is made with pretax dollars, you receive the immediate benefit of lowering your taxable income—which can lower your income tax liability. Once the $100 is in the 401(k) account, it earns 5% after one year. Here's the big benefit: all assets in the account grow tax deferred. Because of this, you get to take advantage of what is referred to as triple compounding:

- Your principal of $100 earns interest

- Your $5 interest earns interest

- Your money that would have been paid in taxes earns interest

You would be amazed at what wonders an investment account can perform if it's not subject to either income tax or capital gains taxes. Trust me, I've seen it first-hand. I have heard countless stories from clients who started 401(k) or 403(b) accounts with their first employers. They stayed with the company for a few years and literally forgot about those retirement accounts. Countless years later, they would receive a statement showing a number that they couldn't believe. And this growth came from an account they contributed to for a few years that was allowed to continue growing on a tax deferred basis. It's not magic, it's financial planning and the power of compounding interest in a tax deferred account.

For all the great benefits of qualified retirement accounts and IRA's, there are some drawbacks. These accounts make for great retirement accumulation tools, but there are strings attached. Here are some rules that apply to these types of accounts:

- All pretax dollars contributed to the account, when distributed, will cause a taxable event. You will be taxed based upon your current income tax level.

- Most withdrawals from a qualified account have a 10% tax penalty for withdrawals made before age 59 ½.

- Most qualified plans mandate required minimum distributions once the owner of the account reaches age 70 ½.

Qualified accounts were created to provide a tax advantaged means of growing an account over a long period of time. They provide wonderful accumulation benefits, but because they were created for long term accumulation, there are penalties for early withdrawal. The IRS will give you a great growth boost, but they will eventually need to tax those dollars. That is why they mandate distributions at a specific age.

Take advantage of qualified accounts if you can. The IRS doesn't give us many opportunities to grow assets on a tax deferred basis. You can hold the same investments in a qualified account and a nonqualified, and over the long term you will see the dramatic difference in the growth of the asset over time. If you are investing for the long term, it is imperative that you take advantage of all the available financial tools that can help you reach your financial goals in a tax efficient manner. The power of triple compounding inherent in qualified accounts is not only beneficial, it's essential to successful financial planning.

A wise person once told me, "Liars may figure, but figures don't lie." This is especially true when talking about investments and investment returns. An investment that did amazingly well last year or for the last few years can drop in value in a matter of days. Investments do not come with guarantees. Indeed, very little in life is guaranteed. The expectation that all stocks, bonds and the businesses that drive the economy will always do well is a false premise.

Investing is based on capitalism, and capitalism is based on risk. As mere mortals, all we can control in the world of investing is how our money is invested (asset allocation) and what price we pay for those investments. We can decide to hoard our money in coffee cans and bury this treasure in the back yard, or we can choose to invest in the currency markets. We can buy a stock and hold it outright, or we can purchase a mutual fund that charges a 1% management fee.

By working with a financial planner you can look at your available investment options and find the best fit you and your family's needs.

INSURANCE MANAGEMENT

Life is full of risk. Over one's average life expectancy, an individual will encounter countless hazards on a daily basis; nonetheless, it often seems that no one ever expects that the perils of life will affect them personally. Yet we do know that around every corner, and in every life decision there is a potential for loss. And if that loss is big enough, it can negatively alter or completely devastate a personal financial plan. In fact, by not planning for your financial future you run the risk of not reaching your financial goals. It can be argued that planning for the unexpected may be just as important, if not more important, than planning for the expected.

If investments are the "sexy" side to financial planning, risk management is the "practical" side. There are many ways to manage financial risk. Insurance is one way to manage risk and is a popular way to help people protect themselves from certain types hazards and perils.

You may not know it, but you are managing risk every day. Let's walk through a typical day to see how our life choices interact with risk management strategies. You wake up with the assistance of an alarm. This helps you to avoid the risk of waking up late. You may then take a shower. This helps to lessen the risk of offending people with your foul odor. If the trip to the office involves a car, you probably wear a seatbelt to lessen the risk of injury in case of an accident.

One of the first steps to managing financial risk is to determine the level of loss associated with the risk. Once that association is made, we then look at the cost of insuring against the risk. It may be in your best interest to either avoid the risk or self-insure against the risk. In other situations it may be more cost effective to find an insurer that deals with insuring against that type of risk.

Insurance can be a powerful financial planning tool. The concept of insurance is based on pooling the resources of many to pay for the losses of a few. The insurance industry employs specialists, (actuaries), who have the job of calculating how much risk a company should take on and how much it will cost to fund the potential losses. Once the actuaries have done their job, we then have a premium that must be paid for the benefit of owning the insurance.

My goal in this section is not to review every type of insurance product on the market. My goal is to spread awareness and provide insight into the risk management process. I want the reader to be aware of the most common tools that are available and can have the most impact on a personal financial plan. Risk is everywhere. You cannot avoid it, but you can plan and prepare for it.

The first type of insurance that most of us are exposed to is auto insurance. You may have had to pay for this while in high school. Many states require that owners of automobiles carry a certain level of coverage. Auto insurance covers loss due to accidents and/or negligence. When shopping for auto insurance, keep an eye on coverage limits and ancillary features of the policy.

The other popular insurance is property and casualty (P & C) insurance, used to protect against losses in homes and dwellings. There are numerous policies offering a variety of types of coverage available to insure homes, apartments, commercial properties, etc. When looking for the best P&C policy, make sure to weigh the cost of lower deductibles and how that can affect premiums. Be sure to look at the numerous riders. Many people forget to add collectibles and other valuables to their policy.

Also, take a look at the cost of an umbrella policy, a form of liability insurance that can tie your various home and auto policies together, thus providing an extra layer of liability protection over and above the limits stated in your underlying policies. An umbrella policy is one of the most cost effective ways to protect your assets. If you live in a homestead state, your primary residence is protected from creditors. However, if your other personal assets are above the limits stated in your homeowner's policy, those assets may be exposed to creditors. An umbrella policy can provide an extra layer of protection for a relatively small sum of money.

Now that your car and home are protected from risk, it's time to start focusing on the risks that can occur in the lives of the people who make the financial planning decisions. For some strange reason, people will easily spend a lot of money insuring inanimate objects, like a car, boat, motorcycle or home. But they have a tough time insuring the person or persons who create the needed revenue to accomplish their financial goals. This is a challenge that many individuals face. It's also a challenge for financial planners that are working with clients.

There is a long list of reasons why many people are either uninsured or underinsured when it comes to life insurance. Here are some of the top reasons I've heard:

- *I don't need it.*
- *I have enough through my employer.*
- *I can use the money to do other things.*
- *I don't want to leave anything behind.*
- *Life insurance costs too much.*
- *My wife and kids can take care of themselves if I die unexpectedly.*

These are all valid reasons to not own a life insurance policy. But as a financial planner, I believe my job is to help people see not just the *possibility* of what can happen to them financially, but also to plan for the *probability* of scenarios that can happen to them during their financial lifetime. And it's very probable that the unexpected will happen, plus it's guaranteed that we all will die at some point. No one has a date of death on their birth certificate. You purchase life insurance in case you die too soon or unexpectedly, which has a high probability of happening.

My favorite counter-argument is the one I offer to clients who tell me they don't need life insurance, which is usually a knee-jerk response because most people really have no idea what they are worth. They don't look at their earnings potential as a revenue stream that can influence them and their family for years to come. Nor do they factor inflation into the cost of living over a long period of time.

We can take a look at our Jen and Ben family situation to get a better understanding of what I'm talking about. Before we look at an example, though, we should set some basic guidelines for life insurance. There are 3 basic questions that should be asked when looking at utilizing life insurance:

> **1)** *How much life insurance coverage do you need?*
>
> **2)** *What type of insurance do you need (term or permanent)?*
>
> **3)** *How much does it cost?*

If Jen earns $100,000 a year and Ben earns $200,000 a year, they would have a combined gross income of $300,000. That's a good amount of money by today's standards. How much life insurance do they need? The two most popular methods that planners will use to answer this question are "multiple of income" and "principal to generate income."

To examine Jen and Ben's life insurance needs using the multiple of income approach, we multiply the annual income of Ben, $200,000, by a specified number of years. If Ben and Jen have young children they need to get through school and eventually college, they may have a 20-year time frame they would need to replace Ben's income during that period, if he were to die unexpectedly. $200,000 times 20 equals a death benefit of $4,000,000.

This is a very basic approach to determining how much life insurance is "enough," since this method doesn't take into consideration the effect of inflation on a $200,000 salary over a 20 year period. A $4,000,000 death benefit may sound like a lot today, but 15 years from now that may not provide as much purchase power as it does now. It's a start, though, and that's what is important.

Another popular approach to determining life insurance needs is the "principal to generate income" method, which takes a few more factors into consideration. With this method, we're looking to determine what dollar amount needs to be left behind to produce the needed income of the deceased. If Ben earns $200,000 and he believes that his life insurance proceeds can earn 3% annually, he would need a death benefit in the amount of $6,600,000. This money would then earn 3% to provide his family with the income he no longer can provide due to his untimely death.

There is no absolute right or wrong way to go about determining how much life insurance is needed. The main point is that you go through the process of determining how your unexpected death will affect your family, and how your financial plans will be affected. Will those you leave behind be able to carry on with the plans that were initially set out? Will a spouse have to go back to work? Will children be forced to work and lose the focus of pursuing higher education? Can your debts be serviced or settled once your die?

The example we've looked at so far deals with utilizing life insurance as an income replacement tool, and it's a great financial tool for that purpose. The beneficiary of life insurance proceeds does not have to list the death benefit payment as income. Yes, life insurance benefits, for the most part, pass on to the beneficiary as tax free income.

In addition to the advantages of life insurance already mentioned, I've found that this form of insurance can serve as a wonderful estate planning tool as well. Let's say that Jen and Ben are now entering retirement, they're in their early 60's, the kids have made it through college and have become productive members of society. The couple may not have a need to replace income. They've amassed a substantial estate and can easily fund their lifestyle to and through retirement. They can now utilize a life insurance policy to leverage and pass assets to their heirs. By establishing a policy with a lump sum amount of $100,000, they could provide an income tax free death benefit of $250,000 or more to a loved one, depending on the terms and type of policy.

Depending on the size of their estate, they may be able to utilize a "second to die" life insurance policy that would be used to pay for estate taxes upon the death of the second spouse. These types of estate planning techniques are called ILITs, or Irrevocable Life Insurance Trusts. They can be complicated, but if an estate is large enough, these types of plans can provide a substantial amount of capital to either pay for or defray estate tax liabilities.

Term vs. Permanent

Few people look at insurance as a means to get rich, even though it is possible to do so. Life insurance comes in 2 basic flavors, term and permanent. The best analogy I've seen to describe the 2 types is rent vs. buy. With a term insurance policy, you are paying premiums over a specified term for a specified amount of death benefit. Your premiums do not accumulate and build cash value. So, once the term of the policy is completed, you no longer have coverage. However, if you have a permanent policy, your premiums are paying for a death benefit, and meanwhile, you are also building cash value that you list as an asset.

Term policies can typically offer more coverage for a premium that is comparable to the premium for a permanent policy. In making the decision whether to purchase a term or permanent policy, the following questions can provide some guidance:

- *Which type of policy can provide you the most cost effective coverage?*

- *Do you want to use the policy as an accumulation tool as well?*

- *How long do you need life insurance coverage?*

- *How long do you want to make life insurance payments?*

Permanent life insurance policies have some unique benefits. Your cash value pays for your cost of insurance and also grows on a tax deferred basis. In time, as your cash value grows from years of premium payments and appreciation, your policy may be able to pay for itself without additional premium payments. Some people use their permanent life insurance policies to fund their retirement.

Another advantage of permanent policies is that they allow you to take tax free loans against the policy cash value. If these loans are not paid back before the death of the insured, however, they can affect the final death benefit. Permanent life insurance policies typically cover an individual for their entire lifetime. Once approved, you are covered until death or until the policy lapses due to lack of cash value.

Term life insurance policies can provide for a more cost effective means of owning life insurance coverage. This type of policy is widely used by younger families that are looking to maintain coverage for a specific amount of time. The downside to term policies is that when the term is complete, you may have arrived at an age where you're not insurable, or your cost of insurance may have become cost prohibitive. Due to the actuarial nature of life insurance, the cost of insurance is normally lower for younger applicants. The older you get, the higher the cost of insurance, whether dealing with term or permanent life insurance. It's often said that the best time to purchase a life insurance policy is yesterday.

Life insurance coverage obtained through an employer is a cost effective method of acquiring coverage. Most employer sponsored plans do not require any underwriting, and the cost may be covered by the employer as well. The one big drawback to employer sponsored life insurance policies is their lack of portability. Once you leave that employer, you may not be able to take the term policy with you.

Annuity

An annuity is a contract between an individual and an insurance company. Annuities were created to provide lifetime income: a guaranteed income stream for life. When comparing life insurance and annuity contracts, I would tell my clients, "You purchase life insurance in case you die too soon, you purchase an annuity and annuitize in case you live too long." Though the industry has evolved to where annuity contracts can be used as a long term savings vehicle, they were initially created to help people annuitize a financial asset so as to create a lifelong income stream.

There are two basic types of annuities and two basic phases. You can contact an insurance company or a financial advisor and ask for either a fixed annuity or a variable annuity. A fixed annuity provides a fixed rate of return that is based on the claims-paying ability of the insurance company that issues the contract. A variable annuity utilizes various sub-accounts of equity, fixed, or alternative investment vehicles that can be invested in.

Once you've determined the best option, you will then have the choice to fund the contract. If you fund the contract but do not annuitize (convert the contract into an income stream), this is called a deferred annuity. You are deferring or putting off the decision to annuitize the contract until some future date. If you decide to go ahead and fund the contract and immediately annuitize the contract, this is considered an immediate annuity.

With the reduction of many corporate pension plans, life insurance companies have seen a dramatic increase in the use of annuities over the past few decades. As employees enter retirement and find that they will not have a pension, they will look to create personal pensions funded from their personal savings. There are only a few financial vehicles that provide "guaranteed" income during retirement: Social Security, pensions, and income annuities. With the option of a pension sunsetting for most retirees over the next few years, there will be a greater reliance on personal savings to create guaranteed income sources.

There are many types of insurance that can be purchased to help keep your financial plan on track. Health insurance is a key benefit that can be acquired through an employer or through a group plan. Disability insurance can help to replace income due to injury on the job. Long term care insurance can provide income to assist with daily living once you've reached the later stages of life. There are many financial specialists working in these various lines of business who can help you make the best financial decision for your specific situation.

RETIREMENT PLANNING

I could spend countless pages writing about Retirement Planning, but I won't. Getting people "to and through retirement" has been my value proposition for many years. I have tried to explain to my clients that Comprehensive Retirement Planning is extremely important in our day and age. By "comprehensive" I mean that retirement planning has two phases.

The first half of retirement planning is considered the accumulation phase; it begins when you earn your first dollar and become an income generating member of our society. The second phase of retirement is the distribution phase, which begins when you decide to "hang up the boots" and begin to generate an income stream from a source other than a full time job.

The accumulation phase, up to a few decades ago, was pretty straightforward. You started work at a young age, stayed with the same company for 40 years, and when you retired at age 65 they paid you a nice pension as part of your retirement package. Average life expectancy at that point in time was 70, so all you needed was 5 years of income before you passed on.

Now let's look at the current situation and see how retirement planning during the accumulation phase has changed. You start work out of college and take a good paying job. You may last 3 to 5 years at that job before another opportunity takes you to a better job—more pay, better upward mobility, the ability to travel, etc. Over your lifetime you may have up to 10 employers. And statistically speaking, you probably won't be provided a pension from a majority of them. This is because corporations have been moving toward the trend of adopting defined contribution plans like 401(k), 403(b), and profit sharing plans. Most large companies are either freezing or eliminating their defined benefit plans, otherwise known as pension plans. Why, you may ask? It's simple: because they cost too much.

Pension plans work like this: If a company provides an employee a pension, they are funding a retirement vehicle that will have to provide a lifetime income stream once the employee retires. Clearly, if an employee does end up spending 40 years with that employer, the company will have funded this employee's pension all of those years with enough funds to pay an income —upon retirement— that is determined by one of many formulas. That can cost a lot of money.

But the cost doesn't end there for the company. If the loyal employee retires today at age 65, he or she will have a very good probability of spending 20 years in retirement, based on an age 85 life expectancy. That company that used to be on the hook for funding a 5 year retirement decades ago is now having to fund a 20 year retirement. Imagine that company's CFO looking at a workforce of thousands of employees and the financial drain that a pension would have on returns. Hence, pension plans in corporate America are becoming extinct. And guess who has to fund a majority of the assets needed to fund a successful retirement? You!

The corporate cost of pensions and their subsequent elimination, combined with the transient nature of employees, has revolutionized retirement planning. But not necessarily in a good way. The evolution of retirement planning and the concept of retirement in America have made the accumulation phase a very complicated venture in the lives of hard working people. It has made people ask themselves some tough questions. I've heard quite a few over the years; here's a list of the ones that I will cover in this section of the book:

How much do I need to save, to retire comfortably?

I'm not a fan of this answer but I have to say it: It depends. How much you will need at retirement is as unique at your individual financial plan. There are some industry suggestions, such as a rule of thumb that says you should have enough money saved that it can provide anywhere from 70 to 110 percent of your pre-retirement income. But these are generalizations. My personal answer is that you should save as much as you can for as long as you can, and start saving as early as the day you earn your first dollar.

From a financial planning perspective, it is important to set a retirement goal. If you are 35 years old and earn $50,000, you can do some rough math and determine that over the next 30 years (based on a retirement age of 65) you will have to save up enough of a retirement nest egg that it can help you generate between $50,000 and $75,000 during retirement. I'm not going to break out my trusty HP-12C financial calculator for this and get into computing future value or the time value of money; I simply want to show you a ballpark figure. Your personal financial planner can give you specific numbers. In order to get a $50,000 yield at 3% you would need approximately $1.7 million dollars. If you need $75,000 every year, you will need about $2.5 million earning 3%. So from this basic computation, one can say that in order to earn what they have been earning, they would need between $1.7 and $2.5 million, and they would have a 30 year window to get it done.

Now let's look at reality. Based on various studies, the average 55 year old American has $50,000 saved in a retirement account. That's not a typo, you read it correctly, $50,000 saved for retirement. If this person wants to retire at age 65, or in 10 years, they have A LOT of saving to do. This is a scary reality that is facing millions of Americans. And it's one of the reasons why I wrote this book. We need to do a better job of motivating our money!

Many of the important questions and concerns that surround comprehensive retirement planning are rooted in the issues and challenges inherent in both the retirement accumulation phase and the retirement distribution phase. The retirement accumulation phase, though challenging, is relatively straightforward. You need to plan accordingly, spend cautiously, save diligently, invest wisely, and manage that ongoing process. Sound familiar? Because of the overall length of the accumulation phase the savings, and investing components are the main drivers of that phase.

When you begin to transition to the distribution phase, there will still be a need for these components; however, the emphasis will be on managing the assets to generate an income stream. There'll be no more paycheck to save from or contribute to a 401(k). There will be life- altering decisions to be made surrounding Social Security and health care. It's a long list of considerations. I share what I call the "5 Challenges of Retirement" when I work with clients entering the distribution phase.

These 5 Challenges must be addressed in any comprehensive retirement plan:

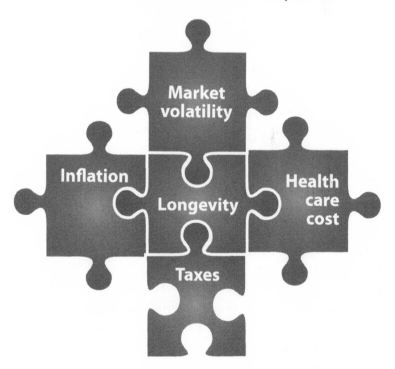

As you move through the various phases of the financial planning life cycle, you will be faced with financial challenges that require action. Having the most appropriate answer that can fulfill your immediate and long term needs is the first step. The next step is to implement that strategy and then monitor the plan continuously to make sure that the plan in place is in line with your current needs. The following is a list of the most popular retirement planning questions that are asked throughout the financial planning life cycle:

What is the best way to save for retirement?

One of the best ways to save for retirement is to use a tax deferred retirement account like an IRA, Roth IRA, SEP IRA, 401(k), 403(b), etc. These types of plans have gained popularity as the retirement plan tool of choice for both corporations and individuals. As corporations have moved away from defined benefit pension plans to defined contribution plans, tax deferred accounts have now become the most common tool for employees looking to save for retirement. The tax deferred treatments of the assets in these types of accounts get the benefit of triple compounding interest, as I mentioned earlier.

Though qualified plans and IRA's are common and familiar, there is a variety of other options available to help save and grow assets for retirement. Many people view real assets like real estate as a long term retirement plan accumulation strategy. Rental real estate, both residential and commercial, can provide both an income stream and capital appreciation. The real estate asset can either be used to generate income throughout retirement, or it can be sold to provide capital that can then be converted to an income stream. There is also the option of participating in what is called a 1031 exchange. This process allows you to exchange certain "like kind" real assets and reduce or defer the tax liability.

Some people view works of art, precious metals, timber or limited partnership interests as suitable retirement accumulation tools. It is important to understand both the pros and cons of any investment strategy that will be used to fund a comprehensive retirement plan. Investments that would do well during the longer accumulation phase may not be the best tool for your retirement distribution phase.

How long will my money last once I'm retired?

No one wants their money to retire before they expire. Of all the concerns that my retiring or retiree clients voice, longevity risk is the most common and concerning. Remember, I mentioned that the retirement accumulation phase is relatively straightforward compared to the retirement distribution phase. Once you've grown your retirement nest egg, the next challenge is to make sure you can make omelets for the remainder of your and your spouse's life.

You may have to modify your lifestyle once in retirement. You may be able to spend more during retirement than was expected. When I initially meet with clients, I routinely ask how old their parents are, or if they've passed on, at what age they died. If dad passed away at age 80 and mom passed away at 90, there's a pretty good chance that you may live just as long, if not longer.

Many financial planners utilize a spend-down percentage of retirement assets to figure a sustainable income strategy. Some believe that if you can maintain your lifestyle from a 4% distribution rate, there is a strong possibility of retirement success. That may be the case. But I believe that strategy is too oversimplified. There are many financial, personal, and emotional factors that contribute to a successful retirement distribution plan. There may be legacy desires that might lend to a lower distribution rate. If you want your heirs to have assets after you die, you may not spend as much while you are alive as you might've spent otherwise. Conversely, if you don't want to leave a red cent to your family, you may want to spend considerably more than 4%.

Your risk tolerance also plays into how long your money will last. With a typical retirement lasting 20 years in this day and age, there will be a need for your assets to overcome the challenges of inflation and market volatility along with longevity. If you were fortunate enough to save up $1 million for retirement, and could earn 4% in a relatively conservative investment portfolio to maintain a 4% distribution rate, that would be great...in today's dollars. But if your $1 million doesn't grow over time and you keep distributing 4%, what will that $40,000 buy you in 5 years, 10 years, or 15 years from now?

That's the double edged sword that many retirees face, once they have made it to the retirement distribution phase. They need an investment portfolio that won't be susceptible to severe market volatility, but they also know that the asset that will be funding their retirement needs to grow to keep up with inflation. It's a tough path to travel. But with consistent and objective financial planning it can be done.

How do I turn my retirement savings into an income stream?

This is the million dollar question when it comes to retirement distribution planning. How do you convert an investable asset into a consistent and potentially growing retirement income "paycheck?" There are a couple of ways to look at retirement income. Many financial planners describe financing retirement with a "3 Legged Retirement Income Stool" analogy. One leg of the stool, or source of retirement income, is Social Security, a second leg is a corporate pension, and the third leg would be personal savings.

These 3 sources combined make up the retirement income stream options that most Americans face. But not all three of these legs will be available to very many Americans once they retire. Many will not have a corporate pension as an option, and among those who don't, few will have a substantial personal savings account that can make up for the lack of a pension.

A client once told me a story that sums up the options that face the typical retiree. He had his "aha" moment regarding retirement income when he was playing golf with some friends at his local golf club. One of his friends spent his entire career working as a government employee. He moved up the ranks and when he retired he was entitled to a significant pension that would essentially replace his income. My client also had a friend who worked in private industry all his life and made a substantial income as an executive. This friend was able to grow his retirement nest egg by saving and deferring income until retirement. He was able to amass an investment account that he could convert to a relatively conservative investment allocation that would generate his income throughout retirement.

My client's revelation was simple: you either work for a company that can convert your earnings power into a pension at retirement, or you work to build a retirement account yourself that can eventually produce a sufficient income stream once you retire. And if you're lucky, you may get to have the best of both worlds.

Many people believe Social Security was created to replace the salary from an employee's working year. This is far from the case. In fact, Social Security only replaces approximately 40% of the average worker's income from their working years. If you are a high income earner, this replacement percentage is considerably lower. Though Social Security does make up one of the legs of the commonly described "3 Legged Retirement Income Stool," it cannot be relied upon as the main source of retirement income. The Social Security program will be under severe financial pressure as the Baby Boom Generation begins to take their hard earned distributions. Without changes to the system, there may not be a Social Security income benefit for those in succeeding generations.

Retirement income planning is challenging, complex, and can be confusing. Due to the large population of Baby Boomers, the need for financial advisors who specialize in the area of retirement income planning is immense. Because of the rise in popularity of qualified plans and IRA's, there is a need to be aware of the income tax ramifications of distributing assets from certain types of accounts. Then there is the consideration of investment taxes on after tax accounts. And then there are the Required Minimum Distributions that must be factored into an income equation once you turn 70 ½. Should you use a Roth IRA or a Traditional IRA to rollover a qualified plan? What about grandfathered provisions in old 403(b) plans that allow for required minimum distributions at age 75 and not 70 ½? What if you decide to work past 70 ½, what can you do with your retirement accounts to defer taxation?

These are all questions and considerations that you may need help with once you reach the retirement distribution phase.

If you don't have the right answer, you could seriously derail your financial plan and run the risk of not having enough money to last you through your ideal retirement.

Retirement Income Planning

When I meet with clients to discuss retirement income strategies, I usually ask them what their thoughts are when it comes to creating an income stream once they retire. Many will mention Social Security; some will mention a pension, while others may bring up a 401k plan. That's a good start. However, there's a lot more to the question. Those suggestions may be the right answer when it comes to the sources of retirement income. But how do you develop a systematic, tax efficient, and strategic retirement income process? It's not easy. And many pre- retirees and retirees are finding that out on a daily basis.

One of the first exercises I share with my clients who are entering retirement is to draw a diagram that illustrates the 3 basic methods of creating income. These methods are the "Bucket System," the "Needs Pyramid," and the "Systematic Spend Down."

The Bucket System is the easiest method for most people to grasp. You have 3 buckets that serve 3 purposes. The first bucket is the "Short Term" bucket to be used to finance 1 to 3 years of retirement expenses. This bucket is funded with short term, highly liquid assets such as savings accounts, money market accounts or CDs. The purpose behind using these types of assets is that they involve little to no volatility. You can feel comfortable knowing that you have 3 years of expenses "in the bank." This allows you to fund the "Mid Term" Bucket with other types of investable assets.

The "Mid Term" bucket can be used to cover expenses between 4 and 7 years down the road, and can be funded with investable assets such as bonds, annuities, or dividend paying stocks. The purpose of this middle bucket is to provide a relatively higher yield than the short term bucket, but still avoid too much market volatility risk.

The "Long Term" bucket can be used for expenditures 7 years or more down the road. This bucket should hold investment assets that can serve as a long term hedge against inflation, such as stocks, long term bonds, real estate, or alternative investments.

The key to the bucket approach is to understand that as you move forward in retirement, assets will need to be "poured" over from the "Long Term" to the "Mid Term," and subsequently to the "Short Term" bucket. This takes some planning and long term monitoring. However, if done correctly, many clients find this method to be quite successful.

The Needs Pyramid method is a good fit for those who require a secure and systematic income stream. Like the 3-tiered Needs Pyramid I mentioned earlier in the book, the base of the pyramid represents the needed expenditures during retirement. The middle of the pyramid represents the wanted expenditures during retirement. And the top of the pyramid represents the wishes during retirement. Once the needed expenditures are determined, we then tie the needed expenditures to a "guaranteed income" source.

Now, there are only a few "guaranteed" income sources available when we're dealing with personal financial planning. Those are Social Security, a pension, or an immediate annuity. The middle of the pyramid, or "wanted expenditures," can be funded with investable assets that provide a "stable income," such as bonds, an annuity or CDs. The top of the pyramid, or "wish expenditures," can be funded with assets that provide "growing income" such as stocks, real estate or alternative investments.

If we take the example of a couple ready to retire, we can use the Needs Pyramid to illustrate how the couple can design their retirement income. If both determine that they "need" $5,000 net monthly to maintain their lifestyle, and that they will receive a total of $2,500 per month in Social Security, they will have a $2,500 need gap. Now, if they will also receive $1,500 per month from a company pension, the remaining gap is now only $1,000 per month.

The only way for this couple to generate a guaranteed lifetime income stream is to purchase an immediate annuity that will provide the $1,000 per month in income. They will have to use a portion of their retirement savings to purchase this income. The remaining investable retirement assets can be allocated in a way to generate stable and growing income.

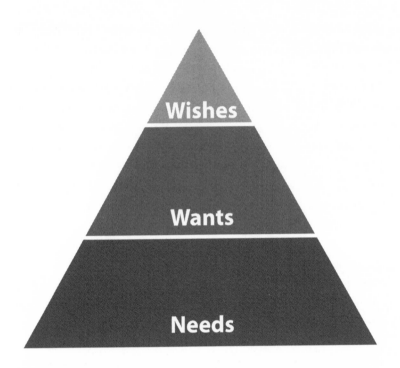

The Systematic Spend Down method is simple, yet it can be the hardest method to manage. Many in the financial planning world have written about a magic spend down percentage. For a good many years, that number was 4%. This means that if you can grow a large enough nest egg, and that 4% growth can maintain your lifestyle (in conjunction with other sources of income such as Social Security and a pension), you should be able to live comfortably during your retirement years.

I have found that there are a few issues with this spend-down method. First, how reasonable is it to expect a consistent annual return of 4%? Second, there are many life situations and desires unique to each family that make a standard spend down percentage difficult to adopt. What if a husband and wife have substantial "guaranteed income" and want to leave a legacy to their heirs? They may only need to spend down 2% of their retirement assets. Conversely, I have seen couples who've amassed a sizeable retirement nest egg and they want to make sure that they use up as much of it as possible. They may desire, and may be able to sustain, a 7% spend down. Then we could take into consideration that different phases of retirement may require less capital usage. A couple may require a 6% spend down in their "Go-Go" years of retirement, but may only need 4% during the "Slow-Go" years, and 2% during the "No-Go" years.

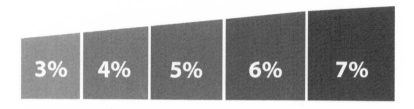

Whichever retirement Income process is chosen, it is important that the client is aware that the distribution phase of retirement requires considerable more planning when compared to the accumulation phase. Working with an advisor familiar with retirement income planning can be extremely beneficial.

What will happen to my retirement savings when I die?

Retirement accounts such as 401(k) and IRA's have some built-in legacy planning tools. These types of accounts have beneficial designations. This means that when the owner of the account dies, the asset passes on to the person listed as either a primary beneficiary or contingent beneficiary. These types of accounts avoid the probate process. Once a death certificate is provided to the custodian of the account and other require documents are submitted, steps are taken to transfer the asset to the listed beneficiary.

These types of accounts can either be incredibly useful tools to pass assets to heirs, or they can cause serious damage to an estate plan. Here are two scenarios that shed light on both the potential benefits and pitfalls of beneficiary designated accounts. Let's bring Jen and Ben back:

Stretch IRA Concept

Jen and Ben are in their retirement twilight years. They have made it through the "Go Go" and "Slow Go" years of retirement. They are now living comfortably in the "No Go" years. Ben dies at the long-lived age of 85, leaving behind a wife, 3 children and 5 grandchildren. Ben was diligent in his financial planning up until his final days. When he sold his successful law firm, he "tidied up his attic" and consolidated all of his qualified plan assets into one IRA. This made his investment management easier, and it also made it easy for Ben to take his required minimum distributions once he turned 70 ½. This consolidation process also made it easier for Jen to manage the account in case Ben died suddenly. Ben made sure to name Jen as the primary beneficiary of his IRA and his 3 children were listed as contingent beneficiaries.

Now that Ben has died, Jen has a few options. Because she is a spousal beneficiary, she can take over the IRA as her own. Because she is over age 70 ½ she must take the required minimum distributions based on her age. She can now list her 3 children as primary beneficiaries and her 5 grandchildren as contingent beneficiaries. There is no taxable event for transferring the IRA from Ben to Jen. Income taxes will be paid on Jen's required minimum distributions.

When Jen passes, The IRA will be distributed based on the percentage dictated in the beneficiary agreement. Her 3 children will then open their own individual inherited IRA's and can name their children as beneficiaries. Jen's children will then be required to take minimum distributions based upon their respective ages. The beneficiaries of the inherited IRA (Jen's grandchildren) will not have the benefit of taking distributions over their lifetime. They will have to take a lump sum distribution.

This concept is called a "Stretch IRA." You are essentially stretching an IRA over the life of generations. This can be accomplished if the beneficiary chooses to take only the required distribution, rather than taking a lump sum distribution once the IRA is passed down. Many people are unaware of this option and take a lump sum distribution, thereby eliminating the possibility of stretching the asset to other heirs. Once assets are distributed from the IRA, they can't be put back in. Sadly, studies have shown that the average inherited asset is totally depleted in 18 months. Imagine working hard to grow an asset for 60-plus years only to have it depleted in less than 2 years.

The Wrong Beneficiary

IRA accounts and 401(k) accounts can be great tools for passing assets on to heirs. As stated earlier, they avoid probate, which can be quite a lengthy and public process. Because of this powerful process, it is imperative that the owner of the contract have the correct and most up to date beneficiary listed on all of their accounts. If you think losing a loved one is a stressful event, imagine losing a loved one and having to deal with both the emotional and financial stress of improper, inadequate, and incomplete estate planning. Here's an example of what I mean:

Let's say that before Jen and Ben met, Ben was married to a woman named Sue; they subsequently divorced. Ben had done some planning when he and Sue were married, believing that he should start a deferred compensation plan along with his 401(k). He also took advantage of the fact that he was young and could get favorable rates on a substantial 30 year term life insurance policy. Ben listed Sue as the primary beneficiary on all of his accounts. Sue had a young daughter whom Ben named as contingent beneficiary.

When Ben and Jen got married,. Ben, failed to update his beneficiary information to reflect his new marital situation. If Ben were to unexpectedly pass away before updating his accounts to show Jen and their children as beneficiaries, the custodian would be obligated to make payment to Sue, who remained the listed beneficiary on the accounts as of the date of his death.

This could be a horrible set of events for Jen to deal with. It could also be costly if she were to retain an attorney to fight the financial battle. The lesson of the story is simple. Make sure all of your beneficiary designated accounts like IRA's, 401(k), life insurance, and annuities are up to date. If not, you could be leaving hard earned money to someone other than you intended.

After Tax Accounts

Passing on after tax accounts to heirs can be efficiently accomplished in a few ways. One of the easiest ways to pass this type of account on and avoid probate is by titling the asset correctly. Spouses can title assets as JTWROS, or Joint

With Rights of Survivorship. If the owner of the account is unmarried, some custodians allow what is called a TOD, or Transfer on Death title, in order to avoid probate.

At this point, I should remind you that a will is a very important document to have. It provides guidance regarding the disposition of assets. However, having a will does not avoid the probate process. Having a trust and holding the assets in the name of the trust is a way to avoid probate. If establishing a trust is not a cost effective method, having the appropriate assets titled to fulfill your legacy planning goals can provide a similar result.

TAX PLANNING

First off, let me disclose that I am not a CPA. The closest I've ever been to being a CPA is reviewing my dad's CPA books when I was a youngster. When my clients need to deal with intricate tax matters, I implore them to consult with their CPA or tax professional. I myself, when it comes to tax planning, know only enough to be dangerous. There are CPA's who specialize in certain area of taxation. Those folks know enough to be deadly.

In this section of the book, I want to cover some basic tax planning principles as they relate to long term financial planning. When it comes down to taxes there are only 3 things can be done: Pay them, Avoid them, or Defer them.

We are all aware that we pay taxes each and every day. There are sales taxes on certain items we buy that can't be avoided. If we want that tall white chocolate mocha, we're going to have to pay a sales tax to get that hot cup of goodness. If you own a home, you have the privilege of paying a property tax. You may have it escrowed or pay it lump sum, but you have to pay for the benefits of having running water, having your trash removed, and having a school for your children to attend. These are the taxes that most of us have to pay, and it is very hard to avoid paying without incurring some serious consequences.

With regard to income tax, investment tax and estate tax, we do have a bit more control. Our daily financial decisions and good financial habits can help us to take advantage of the current American tax structure. We are fortunate in that we can actually take steps to lower our income tax liability. There are financial vehicles that allow you to make tax deductible contributions and take advantage of tax deferred growth. There are also accounts that allow for tax deferred growth and tax free distributions.

Tax planning can be a key factor in accomplishing your financial goals. As you move through the various phases of the financial planning life cycle, you will see that the focus on tax planning is consistent in every phase, and that proactive tax planning from an early stage in life can have a substantive benefit.

Tax Planning Strategies in the Asset Accumulation Phase

During the Asset Accumulation Phase, there are options available to you that allow for the deferral of taxes and avoidance of tax. A company sponsored retirement plan is an account that does both. Your 401(k) or 403(b) plans allow you to make pretax contributions, which lower your taxable income and provide you with the ability to avoid higher income tax liabilities.

For example, if you are a 40 year employee, you are allowed to make a tax deductible contribution to a 401(k) plan. If you have a salary of $100,000 and contribute $15,000 to the 401(k) plan, your taxable income for that year is $85,000 ($100,000 salary minus $15,000 401(k) contribution). Not only have you paid yourself first with the $15,000 401(k) contribution, you also saved yourself or avoided paying $3,750 in taxes (based on a 25% tax bracket) that you would have paid had you not contributed to the plan.

The second tax benefit that is available in the 401(k) plan and IRA's is the power to defer taxation. If the IRS gives you a chance to not pay taxes for a long period of time...take advantage of it! 401(k) plans that offer a company match can have a significant impact on reaching your financial goals. By contributing enough to get the maximum company match, you are in essence getting free money for your retirement. The company is matching your contribution; it's their way of helping you to retire. It helps the company too, as those company contributions are tax deductible to the corporation. If you work for a company that offers a match, be very thankful and extremely grateful. Many small businesses don't offer a company sponsored retirement plan— much less a retirement plan that offers a match.

Because company sponsored retirement plans allow for both tax deductible contributions and tax deferred growth, when distributions from the plans are made they are fully taxable at your current income tax level. Most of these plans will mandate that money be taken out at a specific age.

Tax planning for after tax investment accounts during the accumulation phase can also be instrumental in reaching your financial goals. Most after tax investments do not provide the benefit of tax deferred growth. Unless you are investing in an annuity or whole life insurance policy, you will have to contend with capital gains taxes and income tax. Capital gains taxes are assessed on the sale of any asset that has appreciated in value. There are long term capital gains tax rates and short term capital gains tax rates.

Many people who own investments such as stocks, bonds, mutual funds, and ETF's are familiar with these types of taxes. If you hear the phrase "paper gains" or "paper losses," both refer to the change in the value of the investment. If you purchase a stock for $100 in January and hold onto it over a period of time, you will notice that the value of the stock will change from day to day. If the stock is valued at $110 one day, you have a "paper gain" of $10. If the stock is valued at $90, you have a "paper loss" of $10. You technically have not sold the stock, so the gain or loss is simply showing up on the paper statement you receive, hence the term "paper gain/loss".

If you do decide to sell the stock at $110, you will then have a "real gain" of $10, and will have to pay a capital gains tax on the $10. The rate of the tax will depend on how long you owned the investment. If the stock was held longer than a year, it will fall under long term capital gains rates. If the stock was sold within a year, the gains will be taxed at short term capital gains rates.

The same rule applies to bonds, mutual funds, and ETF investments. One can avoid capital gains taxes by either not selling investments or by offsetting capital gains with capital losses. You should definitely consult your CPA when it comes to matters of capital gains taxes. There are also special tax rates for certain types of dividends paid by company stocks. Your CPA should be consulted for those transactions, too.

Capital gains taxes apply to the sale of pretty much any asset. Primary residences have an exemption limit that prevents people from being penalized if they need to sell their home in an upward market. Any gains over the exclusion, however, are taxable.

Income from certain types of business activities and limited partnerships can be used to offset expenses associated with the respective investment. These unique investment tools can provide some powerful income tax and investment tax benefits. It is highly recommended that you consult with a specialist in the field of interest, and possibly a tax attorney, to get a better understanding of how the accumulation tool will work both in the short term and long term.

Estate and gift taxes are not areas of taxation that most Americans encounter on a regular basis. Estate taxes on the estate of a deceased individual are levied on the value of the estate above the annual exemption limit. As of the writing of this book, the exemption amount is a little over $5 million. This means that if your estate is below that value, you will not have to pay an estate tax. If your estate is valued above the limit, that amount will be exposed to an estate tax. Gift taxes work in a similar manner. You have a lifetime exemption amount that can be given away. Once you gift over that exemption amount, you can be taxed.

Tax management is an essential element of successful financial planning. Taxes are not going away. On the contrary, some believe that taxes and tax structures will increase over time. By understanding that every financial decision has a tax ramification, you will be aware of the need to check how any given financial choice you may be considering will impact your overall financial plan. We either: pay taxes, avoid taxes, or defer taxes. The right combination in your financial plan can have a significant impact on the growth of your assets. The wrong combination can easily take you off the path to success.

ESTATE PLANNING

Again, full disclosure here: I am not an estate planning attorney. I know a lot of good ones, but I do not practice law. I have, however, worked as a trust administrator in a large bank and that experience has provided me with some great insight into how proper estate planning can help pass wealth on to generations of family members.

One of the best "eye opening" experiences I have had happened early in my career, when I was working with the trust administration group. We would routinely have to do trust accountings (which I do not miss doing at all). This process dealt with reviewing the values of trust assets and making sure everything was in good order. As I reviewed the trust holdings, I would note the cost basis of the various holdings in the trust. The cost basis is what the value of the stock was when it was initially purchased.

One of my clients at the time was an older woman who had a significant relationship with the bank. She owned DuPont stock with a cost basis of $2. Do you know how long ago she had to have purchased DuPont stock to have a cost basis of $2? A very long time ago! I later found out that the stock had been purchased by her parents and passed on to her via a trust. It was at that moment that I realized how wealth gets passed on: by proactive financial planning.

My trust client was able to maintain her wealth because of the proactive estate planning that was done by the generation before her. This was accomplished by utilizing the best estate planning tools of their time. They had accumulated substantial wealth and they knew that the wealth they'd built could last a long time and could support their heirs for years to come.

The first step of estate planning is typically a will. A last will and testament is a document that communicates a person's final wishes pertaining to possessions and dependents. The document basically gives direction to an executor and spells out how various possessions should be distributed. A will can also provide direction with regard to the care of dependent children.

If a person dies without a will, they are said to have died "intestate." This leaves the distribution of the estate of the deceased person up to the state-regulated probate process. This process may not be in line with what the deceased person had in mind. Needless to say, having a will is a fairly important part of proactive estate planning. Without a will, assets that you thought were going to a specific person when you die may not happen. The person that you thought would be the best person to care for your children, if not listed in a will, may not be the person that cares for your children if you and your spouse die unexpectedly.

A will can be a very powerful estate planning tool. Though it doesn't avoid the probate process, it can surely streamline that process and make the distribution of assets to your heirs a less stressful process than if there were no will. Depending on the state you live in, the probate process can be a matter of a few months or a few years. In either situation, it is not a fun process. It is filled with emotion, it can be time consuming, and it can cause irreparable family turmoil. Having a last will and testament can eliminate or mitigate a lot of estate planning issues.

Along with a last will and testament, it is also important to have a medical directive or advance healthcare directive. This document provides written instruction as to what medical procedures are to be allowed should the person no longer be able to make decisions due to incapacity or illness. In today's society with the evolution of health care and medical procedures, there is a much higher probability of getting ill or disabled from injury as opposed to dying from an injury. For this reason, it is important to have a formal medical directive in place.

Having Power of Attorney (POA) documents that will allow a family member to act on your behalf is another important element of estate planning. A POA, allows a person to handle your financial affairs should you become ill or incapacitated. These powers can be dictated to suit the needs of the person allowing the POA. One could give POA to a spouse while they are alive and give POA to another individual upon their death.

When structuring a will and medical directives, one of the most important decisions will be choosing an executor. Many times spouses will name each other as executors in their respective wills. However, if one spouse dies, the surviving spouse has to make sure that their executor is someone who will be willing to take on the challenge of the probate process. Many will choose one of their adult children to serve as executor. If this is done, it is important to make the new executor aware of *everything* in your estate. This person will be responsible for handling a lot of responsibilities over a long period of time, so the last thing they want is a surprise. Surprises can set a probate process back for months.

Many clients have asked me what the benefit of having a trust is, and whether they should they create one. This is a great question. And of course, the answer is...it depends. A trust can be a great estate planning tool if you need one. A trust has three basic components:

- **Grantor:** person(s) who places assets in trust

- **Trustee:** person(s) responsible for the trust

- **Beneficiary:** person(s) who benefit from the trust

There are many types of trusts that can provide many types of benefits. The role of a trust is to serve as an instrument that carries out the financial wishes of the grantor through rules established in the trust document. Trusts can be used by individuals while they are alive (living trust), or can come into being once a person dies (testamentary trust). Trusts can be used to own almost any type of asset. A trust can own stocks, bonds, mutual funds, real estate, collectibles, businesses, etc.

"Trust" has become a term that many people associate with rich people. However, this is a false assumption. Trusts are all around us. Corporations use trusts, financial service providers use trusts, and the US government utilizes trusts to help with corporate financial planning. Families use trusts to help with personal estate planning.

Let's look at Jen and Ben in a few examples to see how they could use a trust to help them:

Jen and Ben have made some great financial decisions and have planned for their financial success into their twilight years. They now have a multi-million dollar estate that includes several homes in different states, a substantial investment portfolio, and a successful business. They may consider creating a trust to help them do a few things:

- **Avoid Probate** – A trust can be used avoid the probate process. By having their various real assets titled in the trust name, Jen and Ben can avoid ancillary probate. Ancillary probate occurs when an individual owns assets in a state other than their home state.

- **Provide Legacy Planning** - Jen and Ben can have their investment wishes fulfilled when they die by having a trust that manages their investment assets. This can lift the responsibility from their children, who may not have the desire to manage a large investment portfolio.

- **Reduce Estate Value** - By establishing certain types of trusts, Jen and Ben can implement estate planning strategies that would remove certain assets from their estate. This could help them transfer assets to their heirs prior to their passing, and help them lower their estate tax liability.

- **Family Planning** - If Jen and Ben had children or grandchildren that were mentally or physically disabled, they could utilize a trust that could provide benefits for that disabled family member. Or, Jen and Ben may have "spendthrift" children, and may need to have processes in place that prevent those offspring from inappropriately spending an inheritance.

- **Business Planning** - Jen and Ben could use a trust to help with business succession planning. They can establish certain types of trusts that allow the trust to own shares of the business and pass on the shares to each child upon Jen's and Ben's passing.

There are countless reasons why a person or family may want to establish a trust as part of their estate planning. The situations listed above detail some of the more common reasons. Though having a significant estate may be a reason to establish a trust, it is by no means the only reason or the best reason to establish a trust.

The best advice I can give to my clients is to meet with an estate planning attorney. This should be done at least a few times in your lifetime, when those big trigger life events occur. Most people will start to focus on estate planning once they get married and begin having children. Another trigger event is when children are no longer dependent. Impending retirement often serves as a trigger event that leads to a focus on estate planning. The life trigger that usually gets people to focus on their estate planning, unfortunately, is a change in health.

When you do meet with an estate planning attorney, it is important to have a thorough understanding not only of your needs and desires, but also of the potential impact your estate will have on those you leave behind. Whatever your current concerns or future desires may be, a competent estate planning attorney can help you to structure the best course of action that will help you and your heirs for years to come. Think of estate planning as a way to make sure your financial legacy lives on.

MOTIVATIONAL THOUGHTS/NOTES:

_____

_____

_____

_____

_____

_____

_____

_____

_____

_____

_____

_____

_____

_____

_____

_____

MOTIVATE Your **MONEY!**
Plan > Spend > Save > Invest > Gift

CHAPTER 6

Train Your Money

Amateurs work until they get it right. Professionals work until they can't get it wrong.

- HAROLD CRAXTON

Managing your personal finances to produce long term financial success is not an easy task. It's like having another job. I often instruct my clients to treat their own personal financial plan as if it were a business. It's not that far of a stretch, if you think about it. Every successful business model has a basic structure: generate revenue, work to minimize expenditures, create a profit, and take the necessary steps in between to be able to do it all over again next year.

This, of course, is an oversimplification of business, but the general idea is to make sure that your "personal business" continues to grow. And the only way that's going to happen is if you train yourself to think like a business owner, and apply those business principles to your personal financial situation.

In this section of the book we will look at some successful--and some not so successful —business owner stories. Over the years as a financial planner and financial advisor, I have had the good fortune to work with numerous business owner clients. Business owners are entrepreneurial people. They see opportunity in ways that others do not. This can be a great life perspective, and it can also be a great challenge to financial success. Business owners have to wear two hats. They have to manage both their personal financial plan and their business financial plan. These two worlds often collide and become entangled within the mind of a business owner, and one of their biggest challenges is to learn how to separate the two.

The mindset of the average business owner is that most, if not all of their energy, time and financial resources must go into their business in order for them to succeed. Though it does take tremendous sacrifice and tenacity to start, grow, and hopefully sell or transition a business, there must be an awareness that the business is its own entity, and the owner and owner's family are another, separate entity. Without one or the other there would be no business.

With this division of entities in mind, the business owner must realize that there needs to be personal financial planning that is accomplished with the business entity in mind, and a plan of action for that future time when there will be no business entity. This is a tough sell for many business owners because they need to believe that their business will continue to grow and be profitable. This belief however, is statistically inaccurate. There is a much greater probability that the business will not last as long as the business owner. My job as their financial planner has been to help them plan for the probable as well as the possible. And there is a very high probability that if the business owner is no longer a part of the business, the business will not survive, and vice versa.

There are many situations where the business owner and the business are inextricably tied together. Business owners who provide services, such as doctors, lawyers, engineers and consultants, will have a tough time separating their family financial plan from their business financial plan. There is no machine or system that they can use or replace in their business; they are it. They may have developed a partnership or a corporation as part of their growth process, but if they can no longer function, their income and their business will fail. This can have devastating effects on the family that has been dependent on this business' revenue.

For the business owner who operates a business that is capital intensive, there are pitfalls as well. Though they may have tools that can perform the operations necessary to maintain the business, they may not have the resources to make their business grow should they be removed from the business. Without the business owner's guidance, vision, and dedication, their business may fall apart if there isn't a viable succession plan in place.

Let's take a look at Jen and Ben again, and see what could potentially happen to their family if Ben doesn't make the right business financial planning choices. Remember that Ben is a successful attorney.

In the first situation we look at Ben early in his career as an independent practitioner:

He's decided to start his own law practice. At age 35 he has years of experience under his belt, and a client base that can help him grow his personal practice. Ben anticipates that he can earn $150,000 a year on his own. He may consider starting a PC (Professional Corporation) or LLC (Limited Liability Corporation) or S-Corp, depending on how he plans on growing his firm.

He will need to look at professional insurance and factor in the various expenses associated with owning his own business. One of the key financial tools that Ben will need to have is a key man life insurance policy. This policy would list Jen as a beneficiary. Should anything happen to Ben, the policy would pay Jen a death benefit. She could then use the insurance proceeds to pay off business debts, and replace the income that Ben would have generated over time.

Ben is also aware that because he is his own boss, there is no company sponsored retirement plan that he can contribute to. He now has to create his own plan. Fortunately for Ben, he has options. He considers a Solo 401(k) and a SEP IRA, and decides to start a Solo 401(k). He also rolls over his old 401(k) plan from his former employer. Ben realizes that though his private practice does generate a good income stream, he needs to have a separate investment account that is not dependent on the success or failure of his practice. He also can use the tax deduction from his contributions to the Solo 401(k) and the tax deferred growth.

In the second scenario, we see Ben later on in life with a growing practice:

Ben is now 45 and has grown his law practice to include two partners, Jim and Kim. The law firm is doing great business. Altogether, the firm has 10 attorneys and 20 employees. Ben is a 60% share owner of the firm. Jim and Kim each own 20% respectively. Based on the revenue generated by the law firm, they determine the value of the firm to be $10 million. Ben has invested significant amounts of capital into a new office building that houses the practice. He also derives an income stream from the leases of the other floors in the building. Altogether, Ben's annual income exceeds $1 million.

As part of his succession plan, Ben has decided to implement a few strategies. He has created a buy-sell agreement that is funded by a life insurance policy. This agreement will allow his two partners to purchase Ben's share of the company from Jen should Ben die unexpectedly. This will also allow Ben to purchase the shares of another partner should he die unexpectedly.

With 20 employees, Ben realizes that he needs to provide a retirement plan option to his partners and his employees that will help them along their path to retirement. He decides to start a 401(k) plan with a New Comparability profit sharing plan component. The profit sharing plan will allow him to segment the key employees and provide them with a greater share of the plan contributions. The firm will make the tax deductible contributions to the plan. The 401(k) will have a matching component, and this will allow his employees to defer a portion of their salaries to fund their retirement.

Ben is also concerned about the ability to convert his share of the practice into an income stream at retirement. He learns about an ESOP (Employee Stock Option Plan) and decides that it could be great tool to benefit long term employees, attract new employees, and serve as a method to finance his eventual retirement.

In the final scenario, we look at Ben
at age 65 and ready to retire:

Ben has worked to build a thriving law practice. The firm now has offices in 3 states and a large employee base. Over the years, Ben realized that due to his ever increasing income from his law firm, he could benefit from a deferred compensation arrangement. This non-qualified deferred compensation plan would allow him and a select group of high income earners to defer their current income until a future time, such as retirement. At retirement Ben can convert the deferred compensation plan into an income stream.

Ben has also utilized 1031 exchanges to expand his real estate property holdings. He uses the provision to move his firm from a smaller building to a larger property that can accommodate his growing law firm. With the guidance of his CPA, tax attorney, and financial advisor, Ben finds investments that allow him to grow his assets while being fully aware of the potential tax pitfalls that can befall someone in this income tax bracket. Master limited partnerships, REITs, and other alternative investments are utilized to diversify his overall estate asset allocation.

Ben realizes that he has done well for himself and his family, and he would like to give back to his alma mater, the University of Maryland. Ben has a few options to satisfy his altruistic needs. He could give an outright gift to the university. He could also establish a charitable gift annuity, which would allow him to make a gift of cash or assets in return for a lifetime income stream. He decides on the latter. Upon Ben's death, the university will keep the asset. This gift strategy fulfills Ben's desire to give to his alma mater, while securing a potential income stream for retirement or legacy planning.

With proactive business planning and personal financial planning, Ben can achieve the financial success he has always dreamed of. His business can grow and his family can benefit from the time, energy, passion, and sacrifice invested on a daily basis. The story of Ben may sound fictitious, but it is being lived every day by business owners who focus on what they can do to help both their business and their family succeed.

The 5 Steps to Financial Success apply not only to personal financial plans, but to business financial plans as well. Every business owner strives to plan accordingly, spend cautiously, save diligently, invest wisely, and gift generously for the sake of growing their business. But if the business owner can't follow these steps in their personal finances, it is difficult to transfer the steps to their business plan.

MOTIVATIONAL THOUGHTS/NOTES:

MOTIVATE *Your* **MONEY!**
Plan > Spend > Save > Invest > Gift

CHAPTER 7

See Where You Want to Be

A journey of a thousand miles begins with the first step.

- LAO-TSU

In the world of financial planning, seeing is believing. We want to see that whichever financial solution we implement will yield results. We are all a bit myopic in that way. If there's an immediate issue, we look for the solution that provides a remedy with the least amount of resistance. In this section of the book, I ask that you take a step back and try to get the bigger picture, by looking a little further down your own financial path. The only way that we can effectively plan today is if we set realistic and attainable goals for the future.

Have you ever sat down, by yourself or with your spouse, and honestly discussed where you want to be financially over the next 5, 10, or 20 years? If you have done this — and have done it continually for many years — you can honestly tell yourself what good financial choices you've made and what bad financial choices you've made.

If you haven't spent some honest introspective time with yourself or shared these goal discussions with your spouse, it may be harder to pinpoint how your financial decisions have influenced your life. It's very simple: if you don't have a set financial goal in sight, you won't be able to determine where you're going, and more importantly, you won't know how to get there.

Unfortunately, too many Americans are living like financial zombies. They are simply floating along in this flowing financial river called the U.S. economy. They are trapped by a lack of financial knowledge, overspending, excess debt, and an overall lack of motivation to take control of their financial lives.

But we all know someone who has actually taken those steps needed to take control of their financial lives– and has done amazing things for himself and for others. This may be someone in your family, or it may be a friend or colleague. Don't be afraid to reach out and ask that person to share their story. If you see someone who is living the lifestyle you want to live, there's only one way to find out their secret. Ask them! You may be surprised to find that their answer isn't a life changing gem that you can automatically copy, or flip a switch to implement. This person has been walking a path of thousands of steps that has placed them where they are today.

Just as it is important to have a professional mentor who can provide guidance and insight into climbing your respective career ladder, it is important to have a financial mentor. This is the person in your life who can help serve as your financial beacon through life. This person can be a parent, relative, friend, or colleague. No matter who it may be, it is important that this person truly has your best vested interest in mind, and should want you to be as financially successful as possible, even more than you do. Once you find this person and you have found your beacon, you must then serve as a financial beacon to those in search of financial guidance.

A wise person told me that we need 3 levels of influence in our lives. We need mentors, those who have experienced and endured more than we have, and who are able to provide us with guidance and insight into things that we have not seen or cannot see at the moment. Next, we need peers, those whom we view as equals. These people are the ones we can share ideas with and get a feeling of understanding or dissonance. The last level of influence is comprised of those we can help to influence—usually younger or less experienced people who are looking for guidance.

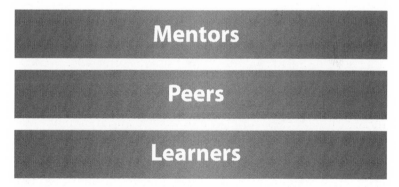

Knowledge and life experiences are like water. There needs to be a constant flow. We all serve as a receiver, receptacle and distributor of this flow. We need mentors to pour their influences and experiences into us. We need peers to share the experiences with. And we need students to whom we impart our life experiences. This time tested process carries on the natural flow of knowledge, allowing financial knowledge to be planted, cultivated, and spread throughout those we influence on a daily basis. This process can help you and those around you become more motivated to make smart financial decisions.

Looking for good sources of consistent, reliable and objective financial advice resources to fill your knowledge receptacle can be a challenge. The financial services industry is an ever changing entity that is filled with good, bad and ugly. It is important to do your due diligence when dealing with matters of personal finance. No matter what someone says, suggests, or implies, the bottom line is: it's your hard earned money. You have to live with the repercussions and ramifications of your financial decisions.

My advice to someone looking for a financial guide in life is to remember that it is imperative that this resource has your best interest in mind. I like to say that this resource needs to have 2 important words at the top of their mind, "vested interest." You must make sure that the resource you are relying on to guide you through a lifelong financial journey has a vested interest in your success. They should want you to be more successful than you ever thought you could be.

This resource should live by the KLT / CPR rules I mentioned early in the book. They must be someone that you Know, Like, and Trust. They must be someone that Communicates honestly with you, provides a Productive service, and Respects you, your family and your goals. A resource that provides consistent and quality guidance and advice will help you on your path to financial success. Not only will they help you, but they will also allow you to pass on your knowledge experiences to those who are in need.

Remember: in the Introduction I mentioned the 3R rule regarding sharing financial strategies with people. The 3R rule is not only a great method to relay complex financial strategies to people. It is also an important test to determine if the financial advice and guidance you are receiving is appropriate. In order for someone to successfully implement and maintain a financial strategy or concept, it must fulfill three goals. The strategy must be Relatable, Retainable, and Repeatable. If these 3 goals are acknowledged and addressed, it will be easier for the financial strategy to be understood, accepted, and shared.

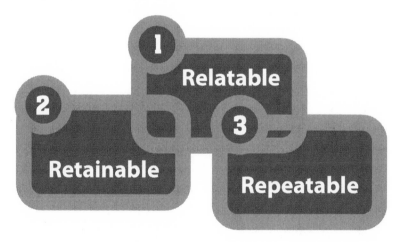

No matter how fantastically wonderful a financial strategy may be, it is of no use to someone if they don't think they need it or can benefit from it. If they can't relate to the features and benefits of a financial solution, they won't care to entertain it— much less implement it. Over my years as a financial advisor, one of the best compliments a client has ever given me was to say, "Mac, you make this complicated financial stuff easy to understand."

That, I believe, is the best thing a financial guide can do for any client: understand their financial concerns and match their needs with the most effective financial tool available— and do this in a way that the client can relate to and easily understand.

Take the following example for how the 3R Rule works.

A college 529 savings plan won't be high on the list of financial priorities for someone who doesn't have young children. However, someone who has 2 young children and is looking for a tax efficient savings vehicle for their college expenses would be very interested in how a college 529 savings plan can help them. This is a person who would very likely be able to relate to that particular financial strategy. Such a client may not know all of their savings options, but the motivation to accomplish this goal is a strong one. So, once he gets a clear explanation of a strategy that will allow him to contribute to an account that will provide tax deferred growth and tax free distributions for qualified educational expenses, this person can then relate to how these benefits can help save long term for college.

Thus, by linking the features and benefits of the financial strategy to the specific needs, desires and wishes of the client, the financial advisor can ensure that the strategy can be easily retained in the client's mind.

Life insurance is a financial service that is often overlooked by many Americans. Statistics show that a majority of Americans are woefully underinsured. For those who are well insured, it probably took someone familiar with the benefits of life insurance to expose both the benefits of coverage and the catastrophic losses that can result from a lack of coverage.

Once you have a life insurance policy, it is easier to own and maintain it if you retain the understanding of what that the policy does for you and your family. By having that life insurance coverage, you know that if you were to die tomorrow, your surviving spouse would be able to pay off the mortgage, pay any debts you may have, pay for the kids' education, or keep a business going. You also know you can provide your beneficiary a tax free death benefit that will replace the potential income that you would have produced were you still alive. By having that life insurance coverage, you can leave behind an asset that can be used to further the dreams and financial goals of those you leave behind. If you can relate to any of these scenarios, you probably already have life insurance. Moreover, if you can relate to these scenarios, it is much easier to repeat your experience and convictions to those around you.

The last R of the 3R Rule is to make sure the strategy is Repeatable. How important is this last rule? It is essential to the flow of financial knowledge. We access information, we analyze it, and then we act on it. Think about the last time you were in a situation that required a financial solution. Who did you turn to? a parent, a friend, a family member? Whomever you turned to, they provided you with an answer based upon their financial frame of reference. The solution that was provided to you by that resource was passed on to that individual by someone else. Your resource person was simply repeating a version of a concept that he or she related to, retained, and now repeated to you.

A great example of the Repeatable rule is the fact that today, the IRA and 401(k) are commonly known retirement plans. The Traditional Individual Retirement Account was created in 1974, and 401(k) plans were enacted in 1978. In this relatively short span of time, the IRA and 401(k) have become probably the most familiar and easily repeated retirement savings tools. Few people know all the details of IRA regulations, such as contribution limits, or the rules for required minimum distributions at 70 ½. But if you were to ask what accounts they have for retirement, either or both terms will be the answer.

The reason for the explosion in popularity of IRA and 401(k) plans is that they fill a relatively universal need. If you're looking for a tax efficient way to save long term for retirement, there are only a few options, and an IRA and a 401(k) are two of them. As corporations moved away from the defined benefit plan or traditional pension plan to fund employee retirement, they began to adopt defined contribution plans, such as the 401(k).

If you work for large company today, there's a very strong possibility that you're participating in a 401(k) plan. After 30-plus years of being in existence, the 401(k) plan has become a central part of the American retirement plan for a lot of people. They can relate to what a 401(k) plan does, they retain the concept of how a 401(k) works, and when asked what is the best way to save for retirement, they will usually repeat, a 401(k).

Not every financial challenge can be solved with just one solution. It would be great if life were as simple as saying, "Here's your 529 Plan, here's your life insurance policy, and here's your 401(k) plan, live long and prosper." But we all know that the only constant in life is change. We change, our family changes, and our financial lives change. That's why it's important to work with a financial guide who is aware of how all of your financial tools work together to keep you on the right path to financial success.

By using the 3R Rule, you can determine how your financial guide is working to help you manage your financial plan. Are they providing you a financial solution that works well for you and your family? Or are they selling you a product that works well for them? Are they trying to ensure that you and your family are financially secure today and tomorrow? Or are they trying to make money off of your financial ignorance?

Your financial guide should serve as both your advisor and educator. I frequently let clients know that there are 3 "Knows" in this world:

- *Things you know you know*
- *Things you know you don't know*
- *Things you don't know you don't know*

My job as a financial planner is simply to educate my clients about the things they don't know they don't know about personal financial planning. My job is to know about these things. The client may know enough about financial planning to be dangerous. It's my job to know enough about financial planning to be deadly.

If I know what steps can be taken to get them to their financial goal, I have to share that information to honestly give them the best opportunity for success. I also need to make them aware of the negatives lurking around every corner that can derail them from reaching their goals. That is the job of a financial guide who has your vested interest in mind. A financial guide shouldn't sell you anything. A true guide simply explains the pros and cons of various financial choices and allows you to make the decision. A true guide motivates you to make the right choice.

See where you want to be. Find the best financial guide that can help you. Follow the path that is paved with healthy financial choices. Share the successes and pitfalls of your financial journey with those in need of guidance. Serve as a motivational force in the financial lives of those around you.

CHAPTER 8

Share Your Story

What you leave behind is not what is engraved in stone monuments, but what is woven into the lives of others.

- PERICLES

One of the biggest issues I see when working with people to develop a financial plan is a lack of communication—between spouses, between children, and between parents and their children. Each scenario has its own inherent issues.

In this chapter we will take a look at the importance of communicating your financial plans and goals to those who will be affected. You may think that open communication about financial goals between interested parties is a no-brainer, but I've seen too many scenarios where a lack of open and honest communication caused severe damage to the financial affairs of entire families. In this chapter I want to share stories of success as well as stories of failure, in hopes that one of these stories may resonate with you. One of these examples might help you make a choice that gets you and your family moving on the path to financial success.

We've been using our fictitious Jen and Ben characters throughout the book to illustrate how financial planning can affect us both positively and negatively. We've seen Jen and Ben experience various financial challenges throughout their respective financial life phases. What we haven't uncovered is how they share their success with each other and influence the lives of others with their choices.

As a society, we are held together by our respective cultures. Each culture is based on the ability to communicate our personal experiences—experiences which are communicated essentially through the medium of stories. Our collective existence is, simply put, a collection of life stories that we've been exposed to over our lifetime.

The reason you speak the way you do, the reason you act the way you do, and the reason you do the things you do are all primarily based upon your surroundings. Your parents, family, friends and peers influence and produce the person you are today. Now, I'm not implying that we are all clones of our surroundings. In fact, our ability to choose to act, or not act, is what makes us such powerful beings. But if you examine how cultures around the world are developed, you will see that influences such as language, food, and religion are powerful ones.

Financial behaviors are also very powerful influences in our respective cultures. The propensity to spend, save, and invest is generally based on the prevailing ideals of the community you live in. Financial decisions lead to financial choices, which lead to financial habits and, in turn, inevitably lead to either financial success or failure. But why do people make the financial choices they make?

If we base our answer on the presumption that we are all a product of a collection of life stories learned from those who make up our circle of influence, then one of the primary influences on our financial choices is our parents.

As children, we are constantly and consistently being influenced by those around us. From our early stages in life we begin to create frames of reference around what is right and wrong. We are told what we should and shouldn't do based upon the prevailing culture we are exposed to. Our behavioral foundation is set, some say, by the age of 7.

If this is true, we have to ask ourselves these questions: If you are a parent, what personal financial training are you exposing your child to? And if you are indeed doing this kind of training, at what age are you exposing your child to the importance of managing their own personal finances? If you're not exposing your child to the importance of personal financial management, why aren't you? What financial stories are you, or aren't you sharing with your children?

If you're not a parent, what financial stories are you sharing with those in your circle of influence? Are you talking about personal financial management with those close to you? If not, why not?

In order to be successful at personal financial planning, one needs to focus on that aspect of one's life. In order for that to happen, it needs to be a priority in your life. And the things that are priorities in our lives are things that we hold as valuable. So if we can find value in financial planning, hold it as a priority in our lives, and focus on the process of planning, we can achieve amazing results individually and as a society. This process needs to start at home, and it needs to start at an early age if it is to truly become an innate part of a person's behavioral process.

You may be asking the million-dollar question: If I don't know much about personal financial planning, how can I teach others? The answer is that it's never too late to start learning. Granted, if you started funding your retirement plan at age 18, you would have a lot more money saved up at age 65 than if you hadn't done so. But, if your started to focus on retirement planning at age 40 and began to prioritize your finances at that age, you would still have 25 years to plan and save before you reached 65. You started later, but at least you started.

One of the most memorable experiences I've had as an advisor occurred at a company employee enrollment meeting. I was there to help set up a retirement plan for this company, which had about 150 employees. During the meeting, you could see the various cohorts of employees huddle together. The younger folks were sitting to the left and the older employees were gathered to the right.

I began my presentation and explained the power of planning, compounding interest, tax deferral, and other aspects of retirement planning. Meanwhile, the group of younger employees was chatting away. They were probably attending the meeting because they were required to. In their minds, probably, retirement planning was for old people.

I continued to talk until my junior advisor grabbed my attention midway through my presentation, indicating an older gentleman who had stood up and raised his hand. I acknowledged him, expecting him to ask me a question. To my surprise, however, he didn't want to address me. He had something to say to the loud, non-attentive young folks.

He said, "You young kids are here to learn about how you can save for retirement. This gentleman is trying to help you. He's trying to teach you. He's trying to give you information that can change your life. But all you're doing is being disruptive. Listen to what he has to say. If I had done what he's saying to do when I was your age, I wouldn't be standing here. I'd be retired by now!"

The young section didn't make a sound the rest of the presentation. And I remain hopeful that the message resonated with a few of the younger employees. This older gentleman was not afraid to share his story. Whether you have experienced success or failure in personal financial planning, you must be able to share your story so that others can either learn to follow your example or learn to avoid it.

COMMUNICATE THE ESTATE

I mentioned in an earlier chapter that the average inheritance is depleted within 18 months. What do you think is the reason behind this sad statistic? I can tell you that the main reason inherited assets are depleted so quickly is a lack of communication. The generation that created the wealth either didn't tell the next generation about the wealth, or they didn't tell them how long or how hard it was to build up the estate. Either scenario is a recipe for disaster.

Let look at what might happen to Jen and Ben's significant estate, which they've worked hard to build over a lifetime, if they don't tell their children about it while they're still alive. Regarding this type of communication, there is a misguided belief that some wealthy families hold. It goes like this: the parents believe that they're the ones who built the wealth, and that their children either can't manage the assets or will waste them. This, unfortunately, is a self-fulfilling prophecy. Because if heirs aren't aware of significant family assets, and all of a sudden they inherit this wealth, they are placed in a very compromising situation. Here are some issues they will face:

- *Estate tax liability*
- *Income tax liability*
- *Asset mismanagement*
- *Asset depletion*
- *Future asset transfer concerns*

If the next generation is unaware of the 10-ton truck coming down the road, all the good intentions and great desires of the deceased parents could end up dead like road kill, literally.

I have seen this play out too often to keep count. Dad will die and Mom will inherit the assets. Unfortunately, although Mom did an amazing job heading the household and raising the family, she didn't handle the finances. There wasn't open communication between spouses. That is the first domino that begins the chain reaction. As a result, Mom is now left to rely on someone she doesn't know to help her through an emotionally draining time. Unless one of her children is financially savvy and aware of her options, she's left to her own resources to continue the financial path set by her late husband. If Mom takes money from certain accounts or doesn't take action with other accounts, she can experience some significant financial issues.

If Mom lives a few more years and then passes the assets to the kids, that's the moment when we see the 18 month depletion clock start ticking. If the kids were brought into the loop after dad passed away, they may have been able to get some idea of what their parents' estate looked like. This exposure would allow them to take preemptive steps to assure that the assets pass on with as few issues as possible. But if instead, Mom kept a tight grip on the family's wealth, her children will now be in for a big surprise. And if they don't have the right counsel or financial guidance, the IRS and their lack of financial planning knowledge will cost them dearly.

The other scenario that I frequently see is the family that makes their wealth known to all generations. The issue that may arise with this situation is that the younger generation, though aware of the wealth, is unaware of what it took to build the wealth. They have been afforded a lifestyle that they've grown accustomed to. What the younger generation doesn't realize is that if those same values and the dedication to growing wealth aren't continued, the wealth will disappear. And it can go very quickly if it's not managed properly.

I worked with a client who owned a successful business that had been passed on by his father. The business owner was married to his second wife, and had 4 children, two from each wife. He made sure all of his children attended the best schools, and they grew to be successful themselves. But none of them took over the family business.

His overall net worth before he died was $15 million. He had a will, but he didn't think he needed a trust. He thought his will would be enough, and because his children we well off, there wouldn't be any issues when it came to the disposition of the business. He was wrong.

His wife was named as a 51% owner of the business, and his 4 children would own the remaining 49%. Things went along fine until his surviving spouse died a few years later. The ensuing financial drama was sad to see unfold. There was internal turmoil among the 4 children. The business folded. And what had once been a $15 million estate dwindled to nothing in a matter of years.

Proper estate planning prior to the death of the owner would have provided for a clear and concise plan to transition the successful business for generations to come. He didn't plan to fail, he failed to plan. He knew his business very well, knew how to grow it and how to make his business profitable. But he did not take the needed personal financial planning steps to make sure the business lasted after he passed away.

This scenario is being played out every single day. Business owners know their business, but they are not financial planners. They need guidance just as much, if not more, than non-business owners do.

Stories of financial success arise when families have open lines of communication regarding their financial health and wealth. I often offer to have both husband and wife and their grown children sit in during my planning meetings. I want all parties to be aware of what we're doing, why we're doing it, and how the strategy can benefit all the parties involved.

Connecting the generations through financial planning knowledge makes transitioning assets due to the passing of family members a much less stressful event than what happens when that communication is lacking. Death is not a fun topic of discussion, but it is one of the certainties of life that must be addressed. If you can impart a financial value system to future generations, implement a strategy for transitioning assets, and minimize the tax liability during the transition process, you're ahead of the game.

Here's a strategy I helped a family implement that proved to be extremely valuable:

My client was a wealthy engineer. He was retired, married, and had kids and grandchildren. He and his wife had a net worth of about $5 million, with most of his assets held in an IRA. Because of his lengthy career with one firm, he was fortunate to have a pension that would more than cover their lifestyle expenses.

He knew that once be turned 70 1/2 he would have to start taking required minimum distributions from his IRA, and was concerned that in his particular case, these would be very large distributions. They, in fact would be over $100,000 annually. He knew that he and his wife wouldn't "need" the money; instead, they wanted that money in the IRA account to eventually go to the kids and grandkids.

Because he and his wife had an estate under the exclusion amount, they were not concerned about estate taxes. They were, however, concerned about the income taxes that would be passed on when they died. IRAs are great accumulation tools, but they can be very taxing when it's time to make distributions.

We decided to implement a strategy called IRA Arbitrage or IRA Maximization. The strategy uses an immediate annuity and a whole life insurance policy. This works well when the clients are healthy and are looking for a way to pass on assets to heirs in a tax efficient manner.

Life insurance death benefits are paid to beneficiaries income tax free, as opposed to IRA benefits that are taxable to beneficiaries upon death of the owner. Here's how the IRA Maximization strategy works:

The client can fund the life insurance policy in a few ways. One choice is to take a lump sum out of their IRA policy, pay the taxes and fund the life insurance policy with one payment. This can be a great way to take advantage of tax deferred growth in the life insurance policy and to leverage the lump sum immediately. This could also cause a large tax bill, so consulting with a CPA or tax attorney is suggested.

Another way to fund the life insurance policy is to carve out a portion of the IRA to fund an immediate income annuity. The distributions from the income annuity will fund the annual premiums of the life insurance policy. The income from the immediate annuity will be fully taxable. However, only the relatively small income payments that are distributed in the year are taxed. This stretches out the income tax liability of the carved out IRA over the life of the client, as opposed to a large one-time tax hit when a lump sum distribution is done in one year.

When the owner of the life insurance policy and income annuity dies, the beneficiaries will receive the tax free life insurance death benefit. The beneficiaries may also be able to receive the income annuity payments, depending on how the annuity payments were structured when the income annuity was initiated.

The IRA Maximization strategy worked to help my client strategically pass assets to his children that would have otherwise gone to the IRS.

The strategy, like most strategies, was a good one. But the reason that it went smoothly from concept, to strategy, to tactic, to result was communication. Open communication and realistic expectations, to be more specific. When it was time to implement the IRA Maximization strategy, I asked that the children be present for the meeting. I felt, as did my clients, that it was important to share the strategy with their children. The parents felt it was imperative for the children to know what was being done, and more importantly, why it was being done. By sharing the how, when and why of the strategy, all parties are now aware of what needs to be done when death of one or both parents occurs.

The story and strategy I just shared with you is fairly complex, but the overarching lesson to be learned is that we need to share and communicate our financial stories with those who are important to us. From a concept as simple as budgeting to one as complex as managing qualified stock options, there needs to be open communication within the family unit. There needs to be a habit of sharing the values and benefits of proactive personal financial planning.

By continually sharing stories of financial success and failure, families can perpetuate their good financial habits and modify their bad financial habits. Sharing stories of spending cautiously, saving diligently, investing wisely, and gifting generously will prepare those around you for financial success. These elements will serve as the financial foundation for future success.

In Closing

Based on the words of Lou Holtz, Motivation is only one part of a formula for success. However, it is the driving force behind our daily actions. We all have the ability to manage our personal finances, and we all have our own attitudes toward money. What we do with our money on a daily basis will determine not only our own destinies, but the destinies of those around us.

There is no perfect way to plan our lives. There is no perfect way to manage money. There is, however, overwhelming evidence that shows we do have control over our financial destiny. It's a long journey through life, and that journey is filled with challenges. If we can learn from those who have travelled before us, and share stories of success and failure, we can create a path of success for ourselves and those we care about the most.

A dear and departed friend once told me that we are in our lives for either a reason, a season, or a lifetime. These words have driven me to help people in any way I can, throughout my career. Someone may come to me about a financial planning concern, and I may enter their life for that single reason. I may help a family plan for their child's college or help a business owner set up a retirement plan. No matter whom I help, I give my best and work to make that person's life better.

My motivation is simple. I am driven every day by the ability to help the people I encounter and to ensure that they have more knowledge and awareness of their personal finances after they have met with me. I may not be able to help everyone, but I can help anyone. This deep desire to impact the financial lives of those around me is the fire that drove me to write this book. My only desire is that my words, my stories and my journey in life can help someone for a reason, a season, or a lifetime. The journey continues...

Watch your thoughts, for they become words.
Choose your words, for they become actions.
Understand your actions, for they become habits.
Study your habits, for they will become your character.
Develop your character, for it becomes your destiny.
- ANONYMOUS

About the Author

Mac Gardner, an advisor with more than 17 years of experience in the financial services industry, specializes in investment management, retirement planning and estate planning as well as comprehensive wealth management. Financial success achieved through knowledge, planning and a disciplined approach to managing wealth is something he firmly believes in.

His knack for making complex financial strategies easy to understand and his approachable demeanor put clients at ease. As he listens to clients' life stories, he picks up on ideas that help define their financial destiny through planning.

His previous experience includes management and vice president positions at firms such as USAA Wealth Management, TIAA-CREF Wealth Management, Bank of America, The Hartford and SunTrust Securities. At these firms he gained expertise in insurance planning, banking, investment management, retirement planning and trust administration. This exposure to various financial disciplines informs his comprehensive financial strategies.

Mac earned a Bachelor of Arts in government and politics with a minor in economics from the University of Maryland.

A variety of professional designations round out his formal education. He has earned the CERTIFIED FINANCIAL PLANNER™ designation, which requires continuing education and a commitment to professionalism and high ethical standards. He has also earned Chartered Retirement Plans Specialist® and Chartered Retirement Planning Counselor® designations from the College for Financial Planning. He draws on this expertise in writing about financial planning for publications and media outlets.

Mac lives in Houston with his wife, Janil; they have two children.

www.motivateyourmoney.com

contact@motivateyourmoney.com

Made in the USA
Middletown, DE
12 February 2022

61014743R00106